PENGUIN CLASSICS

THE KURAL

TIRUVALLUVAR, one of the greatest poets in Tamil classical literature, probably lived and wrote between the second century BC and the eighth century AD.

Some scholars believe that Tiruvalluvar belonged to the weaver caste, others think he was the chieftain-king of Valluvanadu in India's deep south. A third version has it that he was born of a Brahmin father and a Harijan mother. His birthplace by tradition is held to be Mylapore in the city of Madras where there is a temple dedicated to him.

There is evidence that Tiruvalluvar was influenced by the works of other literary giants of ancient India – Manu's *Dharmasastra*, Kamandaka's *Nitisara*, Kautilya's *Arthasastra* and certain ayurvedic treatises, all of which were written in Sanskrit. Be that as it may, Tiruvalluvar's genius lay in his use of Tamil to create the striking imagery, aphorisms and poetry of the *Kural*.

The *Kural*, comprising 1,330 couplets, deals with the first three of the four *purushaarthas*, the supreme aims of life – *dharma* (virtue), *artha* (wealth), *kama* (love) and *moksha* (salvation). However, Tiruvalluvar omitted *moksha* from the *Kural* because (it has been suggested) if the maxims laid down for the attainment of the first three goals were followed diligently, salvation would follow automatically.

P. S. SUNDARAM took degrees in English from the universities of Madras and Oxford. He was a professor of English for nearly forty years. He has written a biography of the noted writer R. K. Narayan and has also translated the celebrated Tamil poet Subramania Bharati into English.

P.S. Sundaram lives in Madras.

D0107147

Tiruvalluvar

THE KURAL

Translated from the Tamil
with an introduction
by
P.S. Sundaram

PENGUIN BOOKS

PENGUIN BOOKS

Published by the Penguin Group
Penguin Books Ltd, 27 Wrights Lane, London W8 5TZ, England
Penguin Books USA Inc., 375 Hudson Street, New York, New York 10014, USA
Penguin Books Australia Ltd, Ringwood, Victoria, Australia
Penguin Books Canada Ltd, 2801 John Street, Markham, Ontario, Canada L3R 1B4
Penguin Books (NZ) Ltd, 182 190 Wairau Road, Auckland 10, New Zealand

Penguin Books Ltd, Registered Offices: Harmondsworth, Middlesex, England

An edition of this book was published privately by the author in 1987
Published in India by Penguin Books India 1990
and in Great Britain and the USA by Penguin Books 1991
1 3 5 7 9 10 8 6 4 2

Printed in England by Clays Ltd, St Ives plc
Typeset in Times Roman

For my friend V.V. John

**Good friends are like good books —
A perpetual delight.**

Kural : 783

Acknowledgements

My understanding of the *Kural* owes a lot to V.M. Gopala-krishnamachariar's edition of the book which included an excellent commentary on it by Parimeelazhahar. Parimeelazhahar, the thirteenth century commentator, sounds as terse and obscure in his rendering of the *Kural* as Valluvar himself, but Gopala-krishnamachariar's edition is a great boon as he uses simple and modernized Tamil.

Also helpful was an edition brought out by the Dharmapuram Mutt, which comprised not only a commentary by Parimeelazhahar but also by four other commentators who were amongst the ten ancient scholars to have commented on the *Kural*.

There are several English translations of the *Kural* (either in full or in parts) by F.W. Ellis, G.U. Pope, W.H. Drew, John Lazarus, H.A. Popley, V.R. Ramachandra Dikshitar, C. Rajagopalachari (Rajaji), K. Sreenivasan, K.C. Kamliah, Suddhananda Bharati and G. Vanmikanathan. I have consulted all of these and benefitted most from Rajaji's rendering.

The advice given to me by Professor K. Swaminathan, by far the greatest and most perceptive of Indian teachers of English, also helped me. I have also benefitted by one general suggestion made by Professor A.K. Ramanujan. M. Shanmukham Pillai's work in Tamil "The Prosody and Various Readings in *Tirukkural*", published by the University of Madras has been an invaluable aid.

Parts of my Introduction to this book also appeared earlier in the *New Quest* (May–June, 1979) in an article entitled "The *Kural* and its Translators".

Madras   *P.S. Sundaram*
June 1990

Introduction

The earlier Indologists (with only a few exceptions) associated India exclusively with the *Vedas*, the *Ramayana*, the *Mahabharata*, the *Hitopadesa* and the poet Kalidasa. This was a result of the discovery of Sanskrit by the British and German savants in the late eighteenth and the early nineteenth centuries which led to something like a second Renaissance in the world of learning. Sanskrit was hailed as the mother of all the Indo-Germanic languages; or at any rate their eldest sister. Sir William Jones described it as a language "of a wonderful structure; more perfect than the Greek, more copious than the Latin, and more exquisitely refined than either".

However, what these scholars soon came to see was that India was not limited culturally to the Aryan north. The Dravidian south was actually older, in the sense that prior to the Aryan invasion the civilization which spread throughout the country was almost certainly Dravidian. A great deal of this pre-Aryan civilization still exists in the south, and traces of it have been preserved in the earliest surviving Tamil poetry of the Sangam age.

An American missionary, Dr M. Winslow, the author of an admirable Tamil-English Dictionary brought out in 1862, perhaps had Sir William Jones in mind when he made the same claim for Tamil that Jones had made for Sanskrit eight decades earlier. It is, he said

> not perhaps extravagant to say that in its poetic form Tamil is more polished and exact than Greek, and in both dialects (common and literary) with its borrowed treasures more copious than Latin. In its fulness and power, it more resembles English and German than any other living language.

Tamil among all the Indian languages, next only to Sanskrit, has the oldest literary records. But unlike Sanskrit it is a living language. Its continuity is such that a Tamil of today will have less difficulty in understanding the Tamil poetry of the seventh, eighth or the ninth century than an Englishman of today will have in understanding *Beowulf* or *The Battle of Maldon*.

The name *Tirukkural* comprises two parts, *tiru* and *kural*. *Tiru* corresponds to the Sanskrit *Sri* and means "sacred, excellent, beautiful". As an honorific meaning 'Hon'ble' it is preferred by many in the south to the otherwise universally Indian 'Sri'. *Kural* may be explained as something which is "short, concise, abridged". It is applied as a literary term to "a metrical line of two feet, or a distich or couplet of short lines, the first of four and the second of three feet". These definitions are Dr Winslow's and correspond to both the traditional and the actual.

Though the work is popularly known by the form in which its stanzas have been written, its earliest admirers and perhaps even the author himself referred to it as the *muppaal*, meaning three divisions; this definition has to do with the organization of the book into three themes: Virtue, Wealth and Love. These are the first three of the four *purushaarthas*, the supreme aims in life, which every man must seek, the fourth being *moksha* or the release from the unending cycle of birth and death. It is said in explanation of the omission of this fourth, the *summum bonum*, that the proper pursuit of the other three will inevitably lead to the fourth, which in any case admits of no description. There is also a precedent for such an omission in the Santiparva of the *Mahabharata* which mentions only the *trivargas*, the three divisions.

Valluvar, the author of the *Kural*, also invariably has the honorific 'Tiru' as a prefix to his name. Whether Valluvar was the poet's name or that of the sub-caste to which he belonged (determined by the occupation or vice-versa) is not certain. Valluvan was a name associated with a weaver. It was also the name given to a drummer proclaiming a king's orders on an elephant-back. The *r* in Valluvar instead of the *n* as in Valluvan is a plural indicating respect.

Those who could not accept that a non-Brahmin could have produced a work of such great merit are credited with the invention of a legend that Valluvar was the illegitimate son of a Brahmin father and a Harijan mother. His birthplace was by tradition held to be Mylapore, a part of Madras, where there is a temple built to honour him. But, in recent years, Dr S. Padmanabhan has propounded a theory based on epigraphical and other evidence that Tiruvalluvar was probably born in what is now the district of Kanyakumari, in the extreme south of Tamil Nadu, and was perhaps the chieftain-king of Valluvanadu who probably, like Mahavira and Gautama Buddha, turned from royal personage to spiritual thinker. Mylapore might well have been the place of his death rather than his birth.

It is not easy to fix the date of the *Kural*. Scholars place it anywhere between the second century BC and the eighth century AD. Vaiyapuri Pillai, the author of the scholarly *History of Tamil Language and Literature*, suggests that Valluvar probably was a contemporary of the Saivite saint-poet Appar (AD 600). There are also those who think that certain sentiments in the *Kural*—for instance, the sovereign quality of forgiveness and the supremacy of love for all things created—might have been the result of Valluvar's leanings to the preachings of the followers of St. Thomas, who apparently came to India a few years after the crucifixion of Christ. But both Jainism and Buddhism are older than Christianity and the most valuable part of their teachings is compassion. It is therefore, not necessary to attribute whatever is best in the *Kural* to foreign influence.

There is evidence in the *Kural* of Valluvar's indebtedness to Manu's *Dharmasastra*, Kamandaka's *Nitisara*, Kautilya's *Arthasastra* and certain ayurvedic treatises all written in Sanskrit. Valluvar might also have been acquainted with Vatsyayana's *Kamasutra*, if it existed in his time. In his delineation of the romantic pangs of a lover, he is more influenced by the earlier Tamil conventions than by anything he may have found in Sanskrit literature. The proportion of pure Tamil words to those borrowed from Sanskrit or modelled after Sanskrit is much greater in the *Kural* than in any devotional poetry of the Saivite and the Vaishnavite saints of the Bhakti school. But, it is less than those used in the poetry of the Sangam period.

For the text of the *Kural* in its complete form, we were until recently indebted to Parimeelazhahar's reproduction with his own commentary on it. The date of this work is said to be AD 1272. There is an ancient verse which says that there were nine other commentators on the *Kural* in addition to Parimeelazhahar. Of these, the commentaries of Manakkudavar, Pariperumal, Parithiar and Kalingar are now available. Manakkudavar probably belonged to the eleventh century and his commentary is now considered to be the earliest. The word arrangement of Manakkudavar is often found to be more satisfactory than that of Parimeelazhahar. His division of words makes better sense without any sacrifice of the metrical requirements. But Parimeelazhahar, who seems to have been a Vaishnavite, as his references to Nammalwar indicate, won encomiums for his wide and deep knowledge of both Sanskrit and ancient Tamil literature, the sharpness of his mind in detecting the errors of earlier commentators, and both the fulness and the brevity of his own comments.

The text of the *Kural* with the five commentaries by the above-mentioned commentators shows a surprising similarity. The numbers and the arrangement of the chapters is the same, and the chapter headings are also identical. While Parimeelazhahar begins his commentary on each chapter of the *Kural* with a justification for its placement in the sequence, Kalingar makes the justification at the end of each chapter.

---

* *Perunthokai*, line 1538

Except for three stanzas in Book III (Love), which in Kalingar's version are distributed differently, among the chapters in the same book as compared with the other commentaries, the stanzas are all the same in the various commentaries. However, within each chapter there is a variation in the arrangement of the ten couplets making up the contents of that chapter. Each commentator was presumably led by his own sense of logic in the arrangement. As regards difference in the text, according to M. Shanmugham Pillai[*], who has studied the matter carefully, in the 1,330 couplets there are only about 305 variations.

It is a matter of some debate as to whether Valluvar himself was responsible for all these stanzas and their arrangement in 133 chapters, each consisting of exactly ten stanzas, or whether it was the work of some later editor. The rigid adherence to the number ten has often resulted in the same idea appearing in different words in order to make up the prescribed number of stanzas, for instance, couplets 8 and 10 under Chapter I of the Proem. In cases where a topic has not been exhausted in ten couplets, it has been spread over several chapters as for example in 'Friendship'.

A question often raised is whether the 'Proem' was a part of the Kural as it was first composed. V.V.M. Raghaviyengar, a great scholar, was of the view that the four chapters which make up the Proem are in conformity with a prescription in Tolkaapiyam, a treatise on grammar and the oldest surviving Tamil classic. The third book on Love in the Kural certainly owes more to the Tolkaapiyam than to Vatsyayana's Kamasutra.

A string of fifty-three verses called the Tiruvalluvarmalai contains praise from various admirers of Valluvar and the Kural. Their literary value lies in the light they throw on the groupings of the Kural's stanzas. Book III for example is described in one of these verses as consisting of not two divisions as in Parimeelazhahar's version but three. But the total number of stanzas mentioned by many of these authors remains the same—1,330. Since all surviving manuscripts contain these verses and attribute them to one single author viz., Valluvar, he has as much right to his identity as the author of the Kural as Homer to his as the author of the Iliad and the Odyssey.

Ancient writers in Tamil enumerating works of antiquity placed the muppaal among the eighteen kilkanakku—Tamil classical literature that was written after the golden age of Sangam literature. In their reckoning, muppaal was just one among these numerous writings,

---

[*] "The Prosody and Various Readings in Tirukkural" (University of Madras)

practically all of which were didactic. It may be for purely metrical reasons that the *muppaal* is mentioned after five other works headed by the *Naladiyar*. But neither on the basis of intrinsic merit, nor from the point of view of chronology can it come after the *Naladiyar*, which seems even to a casual reader a work derived from the *Kural*. The tendency to moralize is perhaps more ingrained in the Eastern psyche than the Western. But the *Kural* is miles ahead of the didactic pieces with which it was associated, because of the way it comes home to our business and bosoms, its author seldom passing on second hand what he has not himself felt in his blood and felt along his heart.

The *Kural* was among the earliest of the Tamil classics to be translated by the Christian missionaries, both Catholic and Protestant. Fr. Beschi of the Society of Jesus (1700–1742) translated it into Latin; though it is likely that he worked only on the first two books, the manuscript of which "the only one in existence", according to G.U. Pope (1820–1908) is in the India Office Library, London. Francis White Ellis, of the East India Company, who came to India in 1796 (d. 1819) as a 'writer' and rose to become the Collector of Madras, translated 120 couplets, sixty-nine in verse and the rest in prose. His translation and commentary have been published by the University of Madras and run into nearly 390 pages. Amongst others who translated the *Kural* into English are Dr Pope, the Rev. W.H. Drew and the Rev. John Lazarus. There are also versions in the French (Ariel) and German (Graul).

The great attraction of the *Kural* especially for the missionaries was its ethical content. Its first chapter is in praise of God, but the praise is universal in content and thus could apply to any God, Hindu, Jain or even Christian. There are some indications in the *Kural* of Valluvar having been a Jain, but Parimeelazhahar, who seemed to have been a Vaishnavite, didn't appear to have found anything heretical in the verses.

The *Kural's* concern is primarily with the world, a world which is the world of all of us. There is very little here of Advaita philosophy, still less of the transcedental. It is not the work of a mystic but of a down-to-earth man of the world, concerned with the home and the community. But while Valluvar is eminently practical he is no opportunist. He is a statesman not a politician, a realist who is not a cynic.

Valluvar was obviously well-acquainted with the *Dharmasastra* of Manu, but while to the latter, *varna* (caste) was not less important than *ashrama* (a stage in life), Valluvar makes no distinction between man and man on the basis of the caste into which he is born. "Call them Brahmins", he says:

> who are virtuous
> And kind to all that live.

According to him there were indeed two classes of men, the noble and the base. But birth, he felt, had nothing to do with either. The noble, he said, would help others even with his bones. Whereas the base, ruled only by fear and greed, are completely worthless and in a crisis will only sell themselves.

Valluvar knew that virtue was supremely important, but also realized that without wealth, it was seldom practicable. "Will that hunger come again", wails the poor man, "which almost killed me yesterday?" Renunciation he said, was fine, but without householders the ascetics would starve and a good householder was not less worthy of honour than a sanyasi. "Ploughmen are the earth's axle-pin: they carry all the world". According to him, they only lived who raised their own food: the rest were "parasites and sycophants". Learning, he said, made one a citizen of the world, but a shy scholar was useless, and one must live one's learning.

Valluvar had evidently read Kautilya's *Arthasastra*, but there is nothing Machiavellian in his manual for princes. He said that it was not his spear but the sceptre which bound a king to his people—and to the extent that he guarded them, his own good rule would guard him. A king, he said, should choose the right servants after careful trial, and once he had chosen them he should give them his trust. According to Valluvar, to prefer personal loyalty to knowledge and diligence was to court disaster. Nepotism, he believed, was both evil and unwise. He felt that constant interference with the work of the subordinates would only hamper justice.

Valluvar's praise of fame, of daring, of knowing how to wait, scorn delights and live laborious days marks him off as an admirer of energy and action.

> Be born if you must for fame: or else
> Better not be born at all.

> The great do the impossible
> The mean cannot do it.

> A world conqueror bides his time
> Unperturbed.

Valluvar was no ascetic. Napolean, at any rate as First Consul, would have, we may be sure, won his enthusiastic approval!

While the second book up to chapter 96 has traditionally been thought of as meant for kings, whole chapters of it, e.g., Learning, Hearing, Friends etc., apply as much to the man in the street as to a prince on his throne. Whether all these chapters were conceived and carried out by one man who by his literary skill gave it a place in the Tamil language as significant as the *Arthasastra* in Sanskrit, may well be doubted. For all we know, some of these chapters at least may have been later accretions and not all of them by the same man. However, they have a remarkable resemblance to one another in their approach to the theme on hand and the verbal execution.

There were two things on which the putative author felt very strongly. The first was ingratitude: "All other sins may be redeemed, but never ingratitude". The second, meat-eating. Valluvar couldn't understand how anyone could wish to fatten himself by feeding on the fat of others. His picture of all the unslaughtered animals bowing to the man who has spared them recalls, in its quaintness, Bernard Shaw's picture of the cows, the sheep, the hens and the fish that he had not eaten, following his bier when he died, a more pleasing sight certainly than their going two by two into Noah's ark. Valluvar's Jainism (if we are to accept this theory) was probably responsible for his uncompromising stand on this issue, but the actual explanation lies perhaps in his senstivity and reverence for all living things.

As regards wine or toddy, Valluvar has a chapter against drunkenness, but when he writes:

> Love is sweeter than wine—its mere thought
> Intoxicates,

one wonders how such an idea could have occurred to a complete teetotaller.

Valluvar's insistence on commonsense and moderation is a constant refrain in the book. His appeal was always to do or think what was patently beneficial. Why, he wondered, did men stop acquiring knowledge when they knew that learning opened all doors? When one liked pleasant words oneself, he felt, how could one use harsh words to others? He asked, does an envious man need enemies? Isn't his envy enough? Or again: You who sacrifice honour to put off death, how long can you put it off?

Whenever one reads Valluvar's thoughts on men of learning, of accomplished speakers, of friends, of children, of a good wife, the pages actually glow. The third book which Drew thought "could not be translated into any European language without exposing the translator

[13]

to infamy", is a paean to youthful love, its ardours and fulfilment and is as moving as *Romeo and Juliet*, as spotless as the *Song of Solomon*. Its shy and romantic refinement has little in common with the sensuousness of Jayadeva's *Gita Govinda*, still less with the clinical sexuality of the *Kamasutra*.

This sage and serious prince of courtesy can on occasion be deadly in his irony. Two instances should suffice:

> The base are like the gods: They also do
> Whatever they like.

> Sweet indeed is a fool's friendship
> For when it breaks there is no pain.

We must not forget that Valluvar was as much a poet as a teacher. His metaphors came as naturally as the sunrise or the koel's song, fresh and artless:

> The Learned lacking expression
> Are flowers without scent.

> The hurt fire caused will heal within,
> But not the scar left by the tongue.

> The lute is bent, the arrow, straight: judge men
> Not by their looks but acts.

> The lotus rises with the water,
> And a man as high as his will.

> Great wealth like a crowd at a concert
> Gathers and melts.

> Swift as one's hand to slipping clothes
> Is a friend in need.

> A boor's great wealth goes bad
> As milk in a can unscrubbed.

A *Kural* stanza consisting of two lines has always been printed following all the ancient manuscripts with four feet in the first line and three in the second. Fr. Beschi who did so much to bring the *Kural* to the notice of Europe, pointed out that actually many of the *Kural's* stanzas had three feet in the first line and four in the second. This is evident when one notices the rhyme as well as the meaning of a verse. Professor E.J.P. Kuiper of the Kern Institute, Leiden is of the view that in as many as 119 of the 380 stanzas of Book I of the *Kural*, the correct way of printing the stanzas should be three feet in the first line and four in the second.

As conventionally, Professor Kuiper might well describe the *Kural* stanza as a halting measure, literally sesquipedalian, "one-and-a-half". But there is nothing sesquipedalian about Valluvar's verses in the dictionary meaning of the term—i.e., cumbrous and pedantic.

On the other hand, his words are simple, carefully chosen and beautifully set, like captain jewels in a carcanet. Valluvar knew the value of words and didn't waste any. He took delight in rhyme and repetition, pun and alliteration and exploited them to the full to drive home a point

Cling to the One who clings to nothing
And so clinging cease to cling.

is typical in its English of much of the brevity and the wordplay of the *Kural*.

Lytton Strachey said of Alexander Pope, countering Matthew Arnold's complaint that Dryden and Pope were not classicists of poetry but of prose because they lacked a true criticism of life, that Pope's criticism of life was his heroic couplet. It may be said of Valluvar even more truly that his criticism of life is the *Kural* in both senses of the term, the book and the stanza. As in Pope's heroic couplet, the admirable thing in Valluvar's *Kural* is the sense of sobriety and commonsense, of balance and proportion. Valluvar is no bard but a man talking to men, a cultured and civilized man talking to those who can appreciate courtesy and good breeding. Every *kural* is a balance, a pair of scales held up for the reader to scan and judge. "Look at this and that", he seems to say, "and decide". The abrupt ending of the second line almost seems to suggest that it is for the reader himself after looking at both the sides of the scale to make his choice, and bring the transaction to an end. The readers, as with Dryden, are the jury. The writer only puts the case.

Valluvar has been translated by several people but there is no English translation of the *Kural* which is entirely satisfactory. The most devoted and learned of the translators, Dr Pope, chose to render the *Kural* in lines that extend right across the page like pythons. If ever an Alexandrine was needless, these surely are. Valluvar, though he lived centuries ago, is not half so 'antique' as the metre in which G.U. Pope has rendered his song is 'stretched'. Rajaji, the ablest and wisest of India's statesmen, brings to his translation his incisive clarity, but his prose is less concerned with Valluvar the poet than with Valluvar the thinker and teacher. Other translations are mostly pedestrian, when they are not sheer doggerel.

It was said of Valluvar by one of his early admirers that he pierced the mustard seed and poured into it the seven seas. Avaiyar, the grand old dame of Tamil poetry, improved on this by substituting the Tamil word for 'atom' in place of the one for a 'mustard seed.' Those who translate the *Kural* at length do not do it the *least* justice, for its soul is brevity and with it *least* is most just. The poetry, to adapt Wilfred Owen, is in the pithy.

Book I

VIRTUE

(i) Proem

1. In Praise of God

1.

A begins the alphabet
And God, primordial, the world.*

2.

What use is that learning which does not lead
To the blessed feet of Pure intelligence?*

3.

Long life on earth is theirs who clasp
The glorious flower-embedded feet.*

4.

Never harmed are those who clasp the feet
Of the one beyond likes and hates.

5.

The delusions caused by good deeds and bad
Shall never be theirs who seek God's praises.*

6.

Long life is theirs who tread the path
Of him who conquered the five senses.*

7.

None shall be free from carping care
Save those at the feet beyond compare.

8.

The feet of the Lord with the Virtue-wheel
Will help to cross the sea of birth.*

9.

Palsied and useless the head unbowed
At the feet of the God of eightfold virtue.*

10.

The ocean of births can be crossed by those
Who clasp God's feet, and none else.

---

*   Lines marked by an asterisk are explained in the notes at the back of the book.

2. Rain

11.

Rain which sustains the world
Should be deemed life's elixir.

12.

To the hungry, rain supplies
Both food and itself as drink.

13.

Should rain fail, hunger will rack
The wide earth sea-girt.

14.

Ploughmen will not plough
If rain withholds its plenty.

15.

It is rain which ruins men; it is also rain
Which lifts them up.

16.

If raindrops drop dropping
There won't be a blade of grass.

17.

Even the wide sea will be less its self
If the cloud depriving it meanly holds back.*

18.

If the heavens dry up, the very gods
Will lack festival and worship.

19.

The vast world rainless, one may bid adieu
To charity and penance.

20.

If the world cannot do without water
Neither can aught without rain.

3. Ascetics

21.

All codes extol the excellence
Of disciplined self-denial.

22.

To recount an ascetic's greatness
Is to number the world's dead.

23.

Their greatness alone shines bright
Who, knowing both, choose renunciation.*

24.

He sows the seed of bliss who rules
His five senses with wisdom's goad.

25.

To his strength who rules his five senses
Indra, the sky-king, bears witness.*

26.

The great do the impossible:
The mean cannot.

27.

This world is his who knows for what they are
Taste, sight, touch, sound and smell.

28.

The scriptures of the world proclaim
The potent utterance of the great.*

29.

The wrath of those on virtue's hill
Though brief,* must have its way.

30.

Call them Brahmins who are virtuous
And kind to all that live.

4. Virtue

31.

What better investment than virtue which yields
Both wealth and release to the living?

32.

No greater gain than virtue
Or worse loss than forgetting it.

33.

By all means possible, in all ways open
Practise virtue.

34.

A spotless mind is virtue's sum
All else is empty noise.

35.

Envy, greed, wrath and harsh words—
These four avoided is virtue.

36.

Defer not virtue, and you will find in her
The day you die an undying friend.

37.

Why talk of virtue's way? Only behold
The *palki*-bearer and the one who rides.*

38.

Be good, don't waste a day; and so
Block the way to rebirth.

39.

Virtue alone is happiness; all else
Is else, and without praise.

40.

The thing to do is the virtuous deed,
The thing to avoid vice.

(ii) Domestic Virtue

5. Domestic Life

41.

A true householder is a steadfast friend
To the other three orders in their virtuous paths.*

42.

For the ascetics, the needy and the dead
The best help is the householder.*

43.

The manes, the gods, guests, kin and self
Should be one's five chief concerns.*

44.

His line will endure who shuns ill
And shares what he eats.

45.

Love and virtue are the flower and fruit
Of domestic life.

46.

What does he gain elsewhere who treads
The pure householder's path?

47.

A householder by instinct scores
Over others striving in other ways.

48.

His is the greater penance who helps penance
Not erring in his worldly life.

49.

Domestic life is virtue, especially when
It is free from blame.*

50.

A model householder on earth
Is a god in heaven.

6. A True Wife

51.

A true wife she whose virtues match her home
And who lives within her husband's means.

52.

Where wifely virtue is lacking
All other glory is nil.

53.

With a good wife, what is lacking?
And when she is lacking, what is good?

54.

What can excel a woman
Who is rooted in chastity?

55.

She whose husband is her only God
Says, "Rain" and it rains.

56.

A true wife never tires guarding
Herself, her husband and their name.

57.

What cage can guard a woman's chastity
Except itself?

58.

The woman who gets her husband's love
Gains the joys of heaven.*

59.

Not his before scoffers a leonine gait
Whose wife scorns a good name.

60.

A good wife is called a boon to a house
And good children its jewels.

7. Sons

61.

We know no blessing better worth our while
Than intelligent children.*

62.

No harm will befall in all seven births
One who begets blameless children.*

63.

A man's offspring are called his property
As their properties spring off him.*

64.

Sweeter than nectar is a man's food messed up
By his child's small hands.

65.

Sweet to the body is a child's touch
And to the ear its words.

66.

"The flute is sweet", "The lute is sweet", say those
Who never heard their children lisp.

67.

The good one can do one's son
Is to place him in the van of learned men.

68.

A wise son gives joy not only to his father
But to all the world.*

69.

A woman rejoices at the birth of a son—
But even more when he is praised.

70.

The service a son can render his father
Is to make men ask, "How came this blessing?"

8. Love

71.

Can love be latched and hidden? A trickling tear
Will proclaim it loud.

72.

The loveless grasp all; while the loving
With their very bones help others.

73.

The soul, it is said, is enclosed in bones
That human love may be.*

74.

From love, devotion comes; and from that unsought
Priceless enlightenment.*

75.

Bliss hereafter is the fruit, they say,
Of a loving life here.

76.

"Love helps only virtue", say the fools:
But it also cures vice.*

77.

As boneless worms wither in the sun, so too
The loveless in a just world.

78.

A loveless life is a withered tree that would fain
Sprout in a desert.

79.

What good are outward features if they lack
Love, the inward sense?

80.

Love's way is life; without it humans are
But bones skin-clad.

9. Hospitality

81.

Keeping house and gathering gear
Is all to entertain guests.

82.

It is wrong to eat even nectar alone
Leaving your guest outside.

83.

The daily feeding of a guest
Will never end in want.

84.

Fortune will smile on the host
Who plays host with a smile.

85.

Why should he think of sowing
Who feeds his guest before himself?*

86.

Who hosts the passing guests and waits for more
Will be hosted by the gods.

87.

The gains of hospitality cannot be reckoned:
Their worth depends on the guest.

88.

"We gathered and we lost", rue those
Who never entertained.

89.

To have no guests is to want amidst plenty:
Such poverty belongs to fools.

90.

The *aniccam* withers when smelt:
A cold *look* withers a guest.*

10. Affability

91.

Those are sweet words which men of virtue speak
Mingling love with sincerity.

92.

More pleasing than a gracious gift
Are sweet words with a smiling face.

93.

Real charity is a smiling welcome
And sweet words heartfelt.

94.

Want and sorrow shall never be theirs
Who have a pleasant word for all.

95.

Sweet words and humility are one's true jewels;
All else are foreign and none.

96.

Sweet words well-chosen diminish ill
And increase virtue.

97.

Helpful words yoked with courtesy
Breed justice and strengthen virtue.

98.

Sweet words free of meanness yield joy
Here and hereafter.

99.

How can one pleased with sweet words oneself
Use harsh words to others?

100.

To use harsh words when sweet ones are at hand
Is to prefer raw fruit to ripe.

11. Gratitude

101.

Neither earth nor heaven can truly repay
Spontaneous aid.*

102.

Given in time, even a trifling help
Exceeds the earth.

103.

Help given regardless of return
Is wider than the sea.

104.

To the discerning a millet of aid
Is as big as a palm fruit.

105.

Not according to the aid but its receiver
Is its recompense determined.

106.

Do not neglect the friendship of the pure
Nor forsake the props in your need.

107.

The good remember through all seven births
The friends who wiped their tears.

108.

To forget a good turn is not good, and good it is
To forget at once what isn't good.*

109.

Deadly though one's sting, one's one good deed
Remembered acts as balm.

110.

All other sins may be redeemed,
Except ingratitude.

12. Impartiality

111.
Great is impartiality, not swayed
By hate, apathy or love.*

112.
The wealth of a just man stays, and passes intact
To his posterity.

113.
Wealth ill-got, however useful,
Should not be touched.*

114.
The just and the unjust shall be known
By what they leave behind.*

115.
The wise will never swerve, well aware
That want and wealth are fated.

116.
Let him who thinks inequity be warned
That ruin awaits him.

117.
The world will not look down
On a just man's low estate.

118.
Like a just balance are the great–
Poised truly and unbiased.

119.
Equity is words without bias
And comes from a firm, unbiased mind.

120.
A merchant's best merchandise
Is tending other's goods as his own.

13. Self-control

121.

Self-control takes one to the gods;
Its lack to utter darkness.

122.

Guard self-control as a treasure;
There is nothing more precious in life.

123.

Self-restraint taught by commonsense,
Leads to virtue and gains glory.

124.

The steadfast self-controlled towers aloft
Taller than a mountain.

125.

Humility, good for all,
Is an added richness to the rich.

126.

Let a man like a tortoise draw his fire in one birth
And he will forge for himself a shield for seven!*

127.

Guard your tongue if nothing else; for words
Unguarded cause distress.

128.

A single bad word will destroy
All other good.

129.

The wound caused by fire will heal within,
But not the scar left by the tongue.

130.

Virtue will wait with timely aid on him
Who learns to curb his wrath.

14. Right Conduct

131.

Right conduct leads to excellence, and so
Must be guarded above life.

132.

Guard your conduct with care; studies won't give
A surer aid.

133.

Caste is right conduct: and its lack
Makes one an outcaste.

134.

Vedas forgot can be re-learnt; bad conduct
Debases a Brahmin at once.

135.

The immoral can no more earn respect
Than the envious be rich.*

136.

The strong-willed never slack in virtue; they know
What evils flow from a lapse.

137.

Right conduct exalts one, while a bad name
Exposes one to undeserved disgrace.

138.

Good conduct sows good, and from bad springs
Eternal trouble.

139.

Men of good conduct cannot speak ill
Even forgetfully.

140.

Those are fools however learned
Who have not learned to walk with the world.

15. Faithfulness

141.

He who prizes virtue and weal
Won't foolishly chase another's wife.

142.

No sinner so foolish as he who lurks
At the door of another's wife.

143.

Those adulterers are better dead
Who betray friends that trust them.

144.

What price greatness if with least scruple
One desecrates another's home?

145.

The adulterer deems it a trifle
But heaps on himself disgrace undying.

146.

Four things will dog the adulterer:
Hatred, sin, fear and disgrace.

147.

A virtuous householder
Does not covet another's wife.

148.

The manliness that scorns adultery
Is both virtue and propriety.

149.

He merits most on this sea-girt earth
Who will not clasp another's wife.

150.

Even a sinner will be well-advised
Not to covet another's wife.

16. Forbearance

151.

To bear insults is best, like the earth
Which bears and maintains its diggers.

152.

Forgive transgressions always, better still
Forget them.

153.

The want of wants is to be inhospitable,
The might of mights to suffer fools.

154.

If you would keep your goodness intact
Practise forbearance.*

155.

Avengers count for nothing, forgivers
Are prized as gold.

156.

The avenger's joy is for a day,
The forgiver's fame lasts like the earth's.

157.

Though sinfully injured it is best
To desist from evil out of pity.

158.

Conquer with forbearance
The excesses of insolence.

159.

Those who bear a reprobate's rude words
Are pure as ascetics.

160.

To fast and bear pangs is great, but only next
To bearing insults.

17. Envy

161.

Make it a way of life to expel
Envy from your heart.

162.

That excellence is unmatched if one can learn
To be free of envy.

163.

He is unmindful of virtue and weal
Who envies another's wealth.

164.

Ill-deeds through envy will be shunned
If the distress to which it leads is known.

165.

The envious need no other foes—
Their envy is enough.

166.

An envious man who runs down charity
Will see his folk naked and starving.

167.

An envious man annoys the Goddess of Wealth
Who leaves him to her elder sister.*

168.

A unique parricide is Envy who ruins
His father's wealth, and leads him to hell.*

169.

The weal of the envious and the woe of the good
Should be pondered.*

170.

None has gained through envy,
Nor the unenvious ever lost.

18. Covetousness

171.

Inordinate desire destroys the home
And leads to crime at once.

172.

They will not sin through covetousness
Who shun inequity.

173.

They will not sin for fleeting pleasures
Who seek eternal joy.

174.

Their senses conquered, the clear-eyed
Will not covet through want.

175.

What use is a mind which is wide and sharp
If it is driven headlong by greed?

176.

Even he whom grace beckons
Beckoned by greed, will scheme and fall.

177.

Avoid wealth through greed:
Out of it comes no good.

178.

Do not cover another's wealth
If you would keep your own unshrunk.

179.

Fortune will herself seek those
Who, wise and virtuous, are not greedy.

180.

Thoughtless greed leads to ruin,
Sublime content to triumph.

19. Slander

181.

Even to ignore virtue and to sin
Is not so bad as to earn a slanderer's name.

182.

Worse than scoffing at virtue and committing a sin
Is to slander behind one's back and smile to his face.

183.

Better die and save one's soul
Than slander, pretend and live.

184.

Better heartless words to a man's face
Than thoughtless ones at his back.

185.

A slanderer's meanness will betray
His virtuous pose.

186.

A slanderer invites a searching censure
Of his own faults.

187.

Those who cannot laugh and make friends
Can only slander and make foes.

188.

What won't they do to strangers
Who broadcast their friends' faults?

189.

The earth bears a scandalmonger
Only for the sake of duty.

190.

Can there be evil if we can see
Our own faults like those of others?

20. Vain Speech

191.

To disgust people with empty words
Is to be despised by all.

192.

Vain speech in public is worse
Than a wrong done to a friend.

193.

Empty words long drawn betray
The speaker's worthlessness.

194.

Vain and crude speech in public
Is improper and degrades.

195.

Men of worth, speaking nonsense,
Will lose greatness and esteem.

196.

Call him not a man but chaff
Who indulges in empty speech.

197.

Unpleasant words may be spoken, but the wise
Should avoid idle speech.

198.

Men of discernment will not utter words
Of scant import.

199.

Not even forgetfully will the spotless and clear-eyed
Say things without meaning.

200.

Speak words which are useful,
Never those that are vain.

21. Doing Evil

201.
The good are afraid, not the hardened,
To strut in sin's robes.

202.
Fear evil more than fire
As sin leads to sin.

203.
The height of wisdom, it is said,
Is not to return ill for ill.

204.
Avoid even thoughtless ill, or else
Justice will work *your* ill.

205.
Plead not poverty for doing ill
Whereby you will become poorer still.

206.
To avoid sorrow for yourself
Eschew evil to others.

207.
Whatever foes you may escape
Your past will pursue and confound you.

208.
Evil's ill-brood are like a shadow
Which hides underfoot and never leaves.

209.
If you love yourself
Refrain from ill to others.

210
No harm shall ever come to one
Who never strays into evil.

22. Social Obligation

211.

Duty is not for reward:
Does the world recompense the rain-cloud?

212.

The worthy work and earn wealth
In order to help others.

213.

How rare to find in heaven or earth
A joy to excel beneficence!

214.

He only lives who is kin to all creation;
Deem the rest dead.

215.

The wealth of a wise philanthropist
Is a village pool ever full.

216.

The wealth of a liberal man
Is a village tree fruit-laden.

217.

The wealth of the large-hearted
Is an unfailing medicine tree.

218.

Those bound to their community
Even helpless will not slacken.

219.

The want the liberal-minded feel
Is not to be able to help others.

220.

If poverty comes of doing good
One's self may be sold to do it.

23. Charity

221.

The only gift is giving to the poor;
All else is exchange.

222.

To receive, even if sinless, is bad; and to give
Even without a heaven, is good.

223.

Never to say, "I lack" and to give
Mark the well-born.

224.

Pity is painful till one sees the face
Of the suppliant lit with joy.

225.

It is great to endure hunger, but only next
To removing it.

226.

A rich man who removes a poor's killing hunger
Lays up treasures for himself.

227.

Hunger, dread, disease, will never touch
One who shares his food.

228.

Don't they know the joy of giving
Who heartless hoard and love their wealth?

229.

To eat alone what one has hoarded
Is worse than begging.

230.

Nothing is worse than death: but death is sweet
If one can't help the poor.

24. Fame

231.

The only asset in life is fame
That comes of charity.

232.

All the praise in the world is praise
Of those who give.

233.

Save fame unique and towering, nothing stands
Undying in this world.

234.

The gods prefer to the merely learned
Those long-famed on earth.

235.

It is only the wise who can convert
Loss into gain, and death into life.

236.

Be born, if you must, for fame: or else
Better not be born at all.*

237.

Why do the nameless blame those that despise them
Rather than themselves?

238.

To die without leaving a name, they say,
Is to incur the world's reproach.

239.

The earth that bears inglorious bodies
Will *bear* less and less.*

240.

Life without blame is life,
Without fame death.

(iii) Ascetic Virtue

25. Kindliness

241.
The richest of riches is kindliness: mere pelf
Even the mean possess.

242.
Seek and secure kindliness, the aid
Which differing codes prescribe.

243.
The darkness and distress of hell
Are not for the kindly.

244.
Those kindly to all creatures it is said
Need fear no future for themselves.

245.
Our wind-blown world attests that grief
Never afflicts the kindly.

246.
Those who are unkind and do ill, they say,
Must be oblivious of the things that matter.

247.
This world is not for the poor,
Nor the next for the unkind.

248.
The poor may be rich one day, but the graceless
Will always lack grace.

249.
Sooner may the muddled head see Truth
Than the hard heart do right.

250.
When you threaten a weaker than yourself
Think of yourself before a bully.

26. Vegetarianism

251.

How can he be kindly
Who fattens himself on others' fat?

252.

The fruits of wealth are not for the wastrel,
Nor of grace for a meat-eater.

253.

Like a man armed to kill,
A meat-eater does not discriminate.

254.

Grace is not killing, to kill disgrace;
And to eat a thing killed, profitless sin.

255.

Not being swallowed is life; and hell
Will swallow the meat-eater.*

256.

If men refrain from eating meat
There will be none to sell it.*

257.

Know meat for an animal's sore that it is,
And you will not eat it.

258.

The undeluded will not feed on meat
Which is but carrion.

259.

Better than a thousand burnt offerings
Is one life unkilled, uneaten.

260.

All living things will fold their hands and bow
To one who refuses meat.

27. Penance

261.

To bear your pain and not pain others
Is penance summed up.

262.

Penance is for the capable:
For others a vanity.

263.

Is it to aid those intent on penance
That the rest refrain from it?

264.

Through penance, if one wishes
Foes can be routed, friends advanced.

265.

Men do penance on earth
That they may get their heart's desire.

266.

The penance-doer realizes his self, while those
Caught in yearning's net defeat themselves.

267.

As fire refines gold and makes it glow
So pain the penance-doer.

268.

All the world will worship him
Whose soul is his own.

269.

Even death is no bar to those
Strengthened by penance.

270.

The have-nots outnumber the haves
Because penance is not for the many.

28. Impropriety

271.

The five elements will laugh within*
At a hypocrite's lying conduct.

272.

What use is a sky-high pose to one
Who knowingly does wrong?

273.

A weakling in a giant's form
Is an ox grazing in a tiger's skin.

274.

A sinning ascetic uses his cloak
As a bird-hunter a bush.

275.

Those who say they are unattached and sin
Will cry in misery, "Alas!" "Alas!"

276.

There is none so cruel as the lying ascetic
Who lives by deceit.

277.

Like the *konri* red to view but black on top
Are many, ochre-robed but black within.*

278.

Many spotted minds bathe in holy streams
And lead a double life.

279.

The lute is bent, the arrow straight: judge men
Not by their looks but acts.

280.

No need of tonsure or long hair
If one but avoids what the world condemns.

29. Thieving

281.
If you would avoid contempt,
Guard your thought against theft.

282.
The very thought of robbing another
Is evil.

283.
Stolen wealth may seem to swell
But in the end will burst.

284.
The lust to steal will in the end
Give endless trouble.

285.
Those are incapable of other-worldly love
Who plot evil for worldly goods.

286.
They will not stick to virtue
Who love stealing.

287.
The wish to steal, that dark cloud of unknowing,
Will not overtake the virtuous.

288.
As virtue in a good man's thoughts,
So greed and deceit in a thief's.

289.
Those who know nothing but to rob
Will sin and fail at once.

290.
The unthieving gain heaven;
Thieves lose both body and soul.

30. Truthfulness

291.

Truthfulness may be described as utterance
Wholly devoid of ill.

292.

Even a lie is truthful
If it does unsullied good.

293.

Lie not against your conscience
Lest it burn you.

294.

Not false to one's own conscience one will reign
In all the world's consciousness.

295.

Truthfulness in thought and word
Outweighs penance and charity.*

296.

Nothing can equal truthfulness
In getting fame and other virtues.

297.

To be unfailingly true
Is to be unfailing in other virtues.

298.

Water ensures external purity
And truthfulness shows the internal.

299.

All lights are not lights: to the wise
The only light is truth.

300.

In all the gospels we have read we have found
Nothing held higher than truthfulness.

31. Wrath

301.

The real curb is curbing effective wrath;
What matters other wrath, curbed or uncurbed?

302.

Vain wrath is bad, but where it avails
There is nothing worse.

303.

Be wroth with none; all evil
Springs of it.

304.

Is there a foe more fell than wrath
Which kills laughter and love?

305.

Keep wrath at bay if you would guard yourself;
Unchecked it kills.

306.

Wrath is a fire which kills near and far
Burning both kinsmen and life's boat.*

307.

A wrathful man's ruin is as hurtful and sure
As the earth struck with one's hand.

308.

It is better to curb one's wrath
Even against blazing affront.

309.

All things desired are his at once
Whose mind is free of wrath.

310.

Temper intemperate is death,
Wrath given up renunciation.

32. Not Hurting Others

311.

The pure in heart will never hurt others
Even for wealth and renown.*

312.

The code of the pure in heart
Is not to return hurt for angry hurt.

313.

Vengeance even against a wanton insult
Does endless damage.*

314.

Punish an evil-doer by shaming him
With a good deed, and forget.

315.

What good is that sense which does not feel and prevent
All creatures' woes as its own?

316.

Do not do to others what you know
Has hurt yourself.

317.

It is best to refrain from wilfully hurting*
Anyone, anytime, anyway.

318.

Why does one hurt others
Knowing what it is to be hurt?

319.

The hurt you cause in the forenoon self-propelled
Will overtake you in the afternoon.

320.

Hurt comes to the hurtful; hence it is
That those don't hurt who do not want to be hurt.

33. Non-killing

321.

The sum of virtue is not to kill
All sin comes from killing.

322.

The first of virtues in every creed
Is to share your food and cherish all life.

323.

The unique virtue is non-killing;
Not lying comes next.

324.

Right conduct may be defined
As the creed of not killing.

325.

Ascetics fear rebirth and renounce the world:
How much better to fear murder and renounce killing!

326.

Death that eats up all shall not prevail
Against the non-killer.

327.

Even at the cost of one's own life
One should avoid killing.

328.

However great its gains, the wise despise
The profits of slaughter.*

329.

Professional killers are pariahs
To the discerning.

330.

A diseased, poor and low life, they say,
Comes of killing in the past.

34. Impermanence

331.

To take the fleeting for the permanent
Is foolish and pitiable.

332.

Great wealth, like a crowd at a concert,
Gathers and melts.

333.

Wealth never stays; use it on the instant
On things that stay.

334.

A day, so called, if rightly understood,
Is a sword hacking at iife.

335.

Do good in time, ere the tongue dies
With the last hiccup.

336.

"He was here yesterday", gloats the earth over man,
"Today he is gone".*

337.

Men unsure of the next moment
Make more than a million plans.

338.

Like a bird's to the shell it leaves
Is a life's link to its body.

339.

Death is but a sleep, and birth
An awakening.

340.

Can life never have a house of its own
Cribbed ever in its cabin ?

35. Renunciation

341.

As one by one we give up
We get freer and freer of pain.

342.

Renounce early if you seek joy;
Great gladness awaits the ascetic.

343.

Control the five senses and give up
All longings at once.

344.

To give up all behoves the ascetic:
Attachment deludes.

345.

When on liberation's road the very body is a burden
Why take other luggage?

346.

His is the world beyond heaven
Who is free of the delusion of "I" and "Mine".

347.

Sorrows will cling to those who cling
To likes and dislikes.

348.

Those who give up all are saved;
The rest are caught in delusion.

349.

Life's tangle is cut with detachment;
Uncut the thread is endless.

350.

Cling to the One who clings to nothing;
And so clinging, cease to cling.*

36. Realization

351.

Of the folly which takes the unreal for real
Comes the wretchedness of birth.

352.

The pure of vision undeluded
Shall taste radiant joy.

353.

To those freed of doubt and clear
More than earth is Heaven near.

354.

Where a sense of the Real is lacking,
The other five senses are useless.*

355.

The mark of wisdom is to see the reality
Behind each appearance.

356.

Those who have learnt to see the reality here
Will have learnt not to come back here.

357.

Reality once searched and seized
No need to think of rebirth.

358.

Wisdom is that rare realization
Which removes the folly of rebirth.

359.

To one who clings and does not cling
Clinging ills will not cling.

360.

Where lust, wrath and delusion are unknown
Sorrow shall not be.

37. Yearning

361.
Desire, they say, is the seed of ceaseless birth
For all things living at all times.

362.
"No birth again" should be our only wish—
And the way to that is never to wish at all.

363.
No greater fortune here than not to yearn,
And none to excel it hereafter too!

364.
Purity is freedom from yearning
And comes of seeking Truth.

365.
Those are free who are free of yearning;
Others, of all else free, unfree.*

366.
Desire is the great betrayer, and its dread
The best virtue.

367.
To him who uproots desire salvation comes
In the most desirable form.

368.
Where yearning is not, sorrow is not;
Where it is, endless dole.

369.
Where yearning ceases, the sorrow of sorrows,
Joy unceasing shall flow.

370.
Eternal joy is ensured
When yearning ever hungry is expelled.

38. Fate

371.

Favouring fate induces energy,
Depriving fate inertia.*

372.

Adverse fate befools, and when time serves
A friendly fate sharpens the brain.

373.

A man may have studied many subtle works,
But what survives is his innate wisdom.

374.

Twofold is the way of the world—
Wealth is one, wisdom another.

375.

Favourable means prove adverse, adverse help
When fate intervenes.

376.

What is not naturally ours cannot be got,
Nor what is, ejected.

377.

Except as disposed by the Great Disposer
Even crores amassed may not be enjoyed.

378.

That the destitutes have not become ascetics
Is because of their fate.

379.

Why do those who take good luck in their stride
Jibe at bad?

380.

What is stronger than fate which foils
Every ploy to counter it?

Book II

WEALTH

(i) The State

39. The King

381.
Who has these six is a lion among kings:
An army, subjects, food, ministers, allies and forts.

382.
These four unfailing mark a king:
Courage, liberality, wisdom and energy.

383.
A ruler should never lack these three:
Diligence, learning and boldness.

384.
He is a true king who sticks to virtue,
Removes evil, and is spotless in valour.

385.
He is a king who can do these—
Produce, acquire, conserve and dispense.

386.
That king is to be extolled
Who is easy of access and soft-spoken.

387.
The world will yield all to that king
Who is sweet-spoken and liberal.

388.
He who is a just protector
Will be deemed the Lord's Deputy.

389.
That land is safe which is under his parasol
Who hears with patience what may not please.

390.
A light among kings is he who has
Grace, bounty, justice and concern.

40. Learning

391.

Learn well what should be learnt, and then
Live your learning.*

392.

Those called figures and letters, the wise declare,
Are eyes to live with.

393.

Only the learned have eyes—others
Two sores on their face!

394.

It is a pleasure to meet a scholar,
A pain to part with him.

395.

A scholar seeking knowledge stoops and is lofty;
The ignorant never stoop and are low.

396.

A well dug in sand yields water as dug—
So learning, wisdom.*

397.

Why does one stop learning till he dies
When it makes all lands and places his?

398.

The learning acquired in one birth
Helps a man in seven.*

399.

That what delights him delights others
Delights a scholar.

400.

The wealth which never declines
Is not riches but learning.

41. Ignorance

401.

To address an assembly ill-equipped
Is to play at dice without a board.

402.

As well might a child flat-chested pass for a woman
As one unlearned for an orator.

403.

Let him but hold his tongue before the wise,
And even a fool is fine!

404.

The learned will not acknowledge
An ignoramus' occasional knowledge.

405.

A fool's assurance collapses
When engaged in a discussion.

406.

The ignorant are like saline soil:
They are there, but useless.

407.

A handsome man with an untrained mind
Has the beauty of a mud-doll.

408.

The wealth of the ignorant does more harm
Than the want of the learned.

409.

The ignorant however high-born is lower
Than the low-born learned.

410.

The ignorant are to the learned
As beasts to men.

42. Hearing

411.

The wealth of wealths is the ear:
That wealth outtops all else.

412.

When there is no food for the ear
We may think of some food for the stomach.

413.

As gods in heaven are fed through fire
So men on earth are fed through their ears.

414.

Though unlettered, listen; you will find this
A great help in distress.

415.

The counsel of the just
Is like a staff on slippery land.

416.

Listen to the good however little
And gain that much.

417.

Those who have sought and heard much
Will not talk nonsense even by mistake.

418.

The ear shut to learning
Though open is deaf.

419.

Ears strange to refinement
Seldom go with modest mouths.

420.

What matters if they live or die
Whose taste is in their tongues, not ears?

43. Wisdom

421.

Wisdom is a weapon of defence,
An inner fortress no foe can raze.

422.

Wisdom checks the wandering mind
And pulls it from ill to good.

423.

Wisdom grasps the truth
Of whatever and by whomever said.

424.

Wisdom simplifies its subtlety to others
And others' subtlety to itself.

425.

Prudence goes with the world, but wisdom
Is not a water-flower, now open, now shut.*

426.

As the world goes, so with the world to go
Is wise.*

427.

The wise know what comes next—
Fools cannot.

428.

Not to fear what should be feared is folly:
The wise know better.

429.

To the wise with foresight
There are no shocks.

430.

Those who have wisdom have all:
Fools with all have nothing.

44. Faults

431.

Those are truly noble who are free
From arrogance, wrath and pettiness.

432.

To be niggardly, touchy and biased
Are faults in a king.

433.

To one who would avoid a bad name
A millet of fault is as big as a palm fruit.

434.

Guard against error as you would guard wealth,
For error is a foe that kills.

435.

A life that does not guard against faults
Is a heap of straw before fire.

436.

How can a king be faulted who removes
His own fault before seeing that of others?

437.

A miser's wealth unused does not increase
But is lost.

438.

Clinging miserliness stands out
Among other sins.

439.

Never flatter yourself, nor delight
In empty deeds.

440.

Keep your attachments secret,
And your foes' plots will fail.*

45. Elders' Help

441.

Value and secure the friendship
Of the virtuous, mature and wise.

442.

Seek them who can remove present ills
And prevent those to come.

443.

The rarest of rare things is to seek and secure
The friendship of the great.

444.

The greatest strength is kinship
With one greater.

445.

A king's ministers are his eyes
To be chosen with care.

446.

No foe can do anything to one
Who has fit counsel and acts right.

447.

Who can injure a king who employs
Men who can rebuke him roundly?

448.

A king unguarded by trenchant counsel
Needs no foes to come to grief.

449.

There can be no gain without capital,
And no stability unpropped by wise counsel.

450.

Foregoing good counsel is tenfold worse
Than facing an army alone.

46. Mean Company

451.

The great avoid the low in whom
The low find their kin.

452.

The soil colours water, and one's company
One's mind.

453.

Perceptions spring from nature,
Character from company.

454.

Wisdom which seems to come from the mind
Comes really from one's company.

455.

The pure thought and the pure deed
Come from pure company.

456.

The pure-hearted will leave a pure progeny
And bad deeds never spring from good fellowship.

457.

A good mind is an asset to everyone
While good company contributes to glory.

458.

A good mind is good, but is strengthened
By good company.

459.

A pure mind ensures heaven, but even that
Is doubly ensured by good company.

460.

There is no greater aid than good company
Nor worse affliction than bad.

47. Action

461.
Act after taking into account
The cost, the benefit and the net.

462.
Nothing is impossible to those who act
After wise counsel and careful thought.

463.
It is not wisdom to lose the capital
For the sake of interest.

464.
Those who fear disgrace
Will not launch thoughtless ventures.

465.
A thoughtless foray only dresses
The enemy's field for him.

466.
It is ruinous to do what should not be done
And ruinous to leave undone what should be done.

467.
Think and act; to act and then to think
Is folly.

468.
An ill-planned scheme, though aided much,
Will go awry.

469.
Even a good scheme ill-apportioned
Goes awry.

470.
None will approve what is not proper:
Act without incurring scorn.

48. Strength

471.

Weigh the strength of these before you act—
The deed's, your own, your enemy's and ally's.

472.

Nothing is impossible for him
Who knows his task and strength, and is well set.

473.

Many led not by knowledge but zeal
Have perished midway.

474.

The unadaptable, ignorant and proud
Have speedy ends.

475.

A peacock's feather can break the axle-tree
Of an over-loaded cart.

476.

A climber's zeal taking one step more on a tree
Breaks the branch and kills him.

477.

Give within your means: that way
Wealth is preserved.

478.

No harm if income is narrow
If outgoings are not broad.

479.

A spendthrift's life
Is a phantom that will fade.

480.

The limits of his fortune are soon reached
Who is generous beyond his means.

49. Time

481.

A crow can defeat an owl by day:
Kings need the right time to win.

482.

The rope that binds Fortune
Is deeds done at the right time.

483.

What is impossible
For right means at the right time?

484.

The whole world is his who chooses
The right time and place.

485.

A world-conqueror bides his time
Unperturbed.

486.

The backward step of a battering ram
Is vigour restrained.

487.

The wise do not burst with rage—
They hold it for the right time.

488.

Bear with your enemy till the time comes
To topple him.

489.

When the rare chance comes, seize it
To do the rare deed.

490.

Bide your time like the stork, and like it
When time serves, stick your prey.

50. Place

491.

Don't despise your foe, nor start action
Till you find a place to hem in and finish him.

492.

A fortress is a great advantage
Even to men of valour.

493.

Even a weak man will win if he chooses
The right place for defence and attack.

494.

A careful approach from the right place
Will outwit the enemy.

495.

The crocodile wins in deep waters—
Coming out others win against it.

496.

A mighty chariot cannot run in the sea,
Nor a boat navigate land.

497.

With details not neglected and place well-chosen
Courage is enough to win.

498.

A large army in a small place
Is demoralized and ruined.

499.

Men on their own ground are hard to tackle
Even when they lack fortress and strength.

500.

A tusker which defies spearmen
Is killed in a bog by jackals.

51. Selection

501.
Choose your men after the quadruple test—
Virtue, wealth, enjoyment and fear of death.*

502.
Choose one well-born, free of fault
And afraid of sin and scandal.

503.
Even the widely-read and faultless
When scrutinized show gaps.

504.
Examine merits and defects,
Strike a balance, and choose.

505.
A man's conduct is the touchstone
Of his greatness and littleness.

506.
Do not choose men who have no commitments—
Unattached they dread no shame.

507.
To favour the incompetent out of love
Breeds inefficiency.

508.
To choose a stranger untried
Will trouble one's line without end.

509.
Trust none untried, and after trial
Assign without distrust.

510.
Trust without trial and distrust of the tried
Lead to endless trouble.

52. Employment

511.

Scan the good and the bad, and then employ
Those who have done good.

512.

Employ those who widen income's ways,
Add wealth and remove checks.

513.

Loyalty, wisdom, a clear head and contentment—
These four well-possessed are the right qualifications.

514.

Many pass all tests and yet
Change in office.

515.

To prefer personal loyalty to knowledge and diligence
Is not the way to employ.

516.

Weigh well the agent, the task and the time
Before you act.

517.

Assured this man will do this task this way,
Leave it to him.

518.

Having found the man for the task
Make him responsible.

519.

Fortune deserts him who distrusts
A diligent worker.

520.

Let the king be alert, his servants upright,
And the state will not swerve.

53. Kindred

521.
Only our kin stick for old sake's sake
Even in adversity.

522.
Unestranged kinship breeds
Unabating wealth.

523.
The life of an unattached man
Is a pond unpounded running to waste.

524.
The use of wealth is that it draws
A man's kin around him.

525.
Gifts and sweet words enable a man
To be circled by circles of kin.

526.
None has a larger kinship than he
Who is liberal and curbs his wrath.

527.
Crows trumpet their finds and share them—
Gains accrue to such natures.

528.
A king with discrimination
Attracts followers.

529.
Deserters will come back
When the cause is removed.

530.
A king should be careful before taking back those
Who leave him without cause and return.*

54. Slackness

531.

Worse than too much wrath is the laxity
Due to too much exultation.

532.

Laxity kills fame as a hand-to-mouth life
Kills the intellect.

533.

All writings in the world conclude,
"Fame is not for the lax".

534.

There is no fortress for the coward,
Nor luck for the lax.

535.

Too late he repents who is lax
Against impending danger.

536.

Nothing can equal never being lax
With anyone at any time.

537.

Nothing is impossible to a man
Armed with vigilance.

538.

Pursue excellence—there is nothing but ill
In all seven births for the slack.

539.

Remember when drunk with happiness
Those who fell through laxity.

540.

All aims are easy to achieve
To those that persist.

55. The Unswerving Sceptre

541.

Searching enquiry, an impartial eye, punishment as prescribed
Are the ways of justice.

542.

The world looks up to heaven for rain
And his subjects to their king for justice.

543.

The king's sceptre provides the base
For scripture and right conduct.

544.

The king who rules cherishing his people
Has the world at his feet.

545.

The king who rules according to the law
Never lacks rain and corn.

546.

Not his spear but a straight sceptre
Is what gives a monarch his triumph.

547.

The king guards the land, and his own rule
Will guard him if he is straight.

548.

A king inaccessible, unprobing and unjust
Will sink and be ruined.

549.

For a king who would guard and cherish his people
To punish crimes is a duty, not defect.

550.

The king who punishes wicked men with death
Is a farmer weeding the tender crops.*

56. Misrule

551.

A sinful and oppressive king is worse
Than a murderer.

552.

A king's request for gifts is a bandit's demand,
"Stand and deliver".

553.

A king who does not do justice daily
Will daily lose his land.

554.

A thoughtless tyrant will lose at once
His wealth and subjects.

555.

Won't the tears of the oppressed allowed to flow
Wear out a king's wealth?

556.

Just rule stabilizes a king;
Lacking it his glory fades.

557.

How fares the earth without rain? So fares
Life under a ruthless king.

558.

Wealth under a lawless king
Is worse than want.

559.

Where a king is unjust
Rains are withheld.

560.

Cows yield less and the six professions* cease
Where a protector does not protect.

57. Terrorism

561.

Call him king who probes and whose punishment
Is deterrent and proportionate.

562.

A wide sweep and a mild stroke ensures
Enduring power.

563.

A tyrant indulging in terrorism
Will perish quickly.

564.

A king decried as a tyrant will soon lose
Both property and life.

565.

The wealth of one inaccessible and sour-faced
Is no better than a demon's.*

566.

The wealth of one harsh-spoken and cruel
Fleets and dissolves.

567.

Harsh words and excessive punishments
Are a file to a king's iron might.

568.

That king will not prosper who does not
Consult his ministers, and treats them rough.

569.

A king who neglects his defences
Will die of fright in a war.

570.

The earth bears no heavier burden
Than a tyrant hemmed in by fools.

58. Compassion

571.

It is compassion, the most gracious of virtues,
Which moves the world.

572.

Compassion is human; lacking it
Men are a burden on earth.

573.

What use is a *raga* that cannot be sung?
Or eyes without sympathy?

574.

What use are eyes that look like eyes
But lack boundless sympathy?

575.

The jewel of the eye is sympathy; without it
Eyes are but sores.

576.

Like trees earth-bound which cannot move
Are eyes unmoved by pity.

577.

They are blind who lack sympathy;
And those only eyes which have it.

578.

The world is his who does his job
With sympathy.

579.

The rarer action is to sympathize
Even with those that hurt us.

580.

Refinement will drink with a smile
Even hemlock when offered.

59. Espionage

581.

A king's pair of eyes
Are the classics on statecraft and spies.

582.

A king's job is to know in time
Everything that happens to everyone each day.

583.

A king uninformed by spies
Cannot succeed.

584.

Employees, kinsmen and enemies
Are the people a spy should cover.

585.

Spies should always be
Unsuspected, intrepid and close.

586.

Garbed as a holy man a spy should go everywhere
Withstanding all strain.

587.

A spy should know and make sure
Of hidden things.

588.

What one spy has spied
Must be confirmed through another.

589.

Let not one spy know another;
And act when three spies agree.

590.

Never honour a spy in public
Lest your secret should be out.

60. Energy

591.

What is one's own is one's vigour:
Without it what does one own?

592.

The real asset is a resolute mind—
Riches and lands fleet.

593.

Those who have vigour will not lament
The loss of goods.

594.

To a man of unshaken vigour
Wealth will ask and find its way.

595.

The lotus rises with the water,
And a man as high as his will.

596.

Always aim high—failure then
Is as good as success.

597.

The strong-willed are not daunted by failure—
Pierced with arrows an elephant stands.

598.

A weakling cannot gain the world's esteem
For strength.

599.

Huge and sharp-tusked though he be
An elephant fears a tiger.

600.

Energy is a man's wealth: the immobile
Are trees in human form.

61. Sloth

601.

The smoke of sloth will dim and destroy
The light of inherent virtue.

602.

Those who would enhance their birth
Should keep sloth at bay.

603.

A slothful fool's household
Will predecease him.

604.

The ease-loving sluggard ruins his house
And multiplies sin.

605.

The pleasure-junks of destruction are four;
Procrastination, forgetfulness, sloth and sleep.

606.

The slothful will not gain
Even with powerful aid.

607.

The ease-loving sluggard must endure
Censure and contempt.

608.

Sloth enslaves a house
To its enemies.

609.

Inherent defects can be changed
By exertion.

610.

An energetic king can get at once
All that Trivikrama bestrode.*

62. Manliness

611.
Do not give up saying, "It is impossible".
Effort will overcome.

612.
The world gives up those who give up:
Stick to your task.

613.
To the persistent belongs the pride
Of doing good to others.

614.
A weakling's philanthropy is a sword
In a eunuch's hand.

615.
A comfort to his friends and a pillar is he
Who scorns delight and loves labour.

616.
Exertion leads to wealth,
Lack of it to want.

617.
The black elder sister dwells on a slothful lap
And the lotus-throned, they say, attends on zeal.*

618.
Ill-luck is never blamed—what is blamed
Is knowledge without exertion.

619.
Even if Fate will not, exertion will pay
The wages of effort.

620.
Those that strive undaunted will see
The back of Fate itself.

63. Fortitude

621.

Laugh at misfortune—nothing so able
To triumph over it.

622.

Misfortune may rise like a flood—
A bold thought will quell it.

623.

Those whom grief cannot grieve
Will grieve grief.

624.

Trouble is troubled by him who bull-like
Drags his cart through every hurdle.

625.

The man who can defy ceaseless trouble
Troubles it.

626.

Will they whine, "We have nothing".
Who never crowed, "We have much?"

627.

The wise are never perturbed to whom
Their body is but a butt of distress!*

628.

He will never be sad who scorns delight
And takes sorrow in his stride.

629.

He who never exulted in joy
Will not be depressed by sorrow.

630.

To take pain as pleasure
Is to gain your foe's esteem.

(ii) The Limbs of the State

64. Ministers

631.

Call him minister who best contrives
The means, the time, the mode and the deed.

632.

Firmness, concern, learning, judgement and effort—
These five should mark a minister.

633.

To part, combine and reunite
Should come easy to a minister.

634.

Enquiry, deliberate action and advice
Should mark a minister.

635.

A helpful counseller knows the codes,
Is learned in discourse and ever resourceful.

636.

What can oppose a keen intelligence
Combined with learning?

637.

However well-versed in books,
Be practical.

638.

It is a minister's duty to advise aright
Even an ignorant foe to learning.

639.

Better seventy crore open foes
Than one treacherous minister.

640.

The inefficient will leave undone
Even well-planned schemes.

65. Persuasiveness

641.

Persuasiveness is a great gift
Rich beyond all else.

642.

Speech can both make and mar, and hence
Should be guarded well.

643.

Eloquence charms the hearer and fills with longing
Those who have not heard.

644.

Speak fittingly than which there is
No greater virtue or wealth.

645.

Speak so that what you say
May never be gainsaid.

646.

To persuade and gain by what others say
Mark good counsellers.

647.

A good speaker, tireless, unforgetful and bold
Is hard to quell.

648.

The world will run and listen to a speech
Sweet and well-set.

649.

Those fond of talking much
Cannot be brief and faultless.

650.

The learned lacking expression
Are flowers without scent.

66. Honest Dealing

651.

A man's friends bring him worldly goods:
His good deeds all he needs.

652.

Avoid always what does not lead
To fame and virtue.

653.

Those who seek greatness must avoid
What will stain their name.

654.

They will not be mean even in distress
Who see life steadily.

655.

Do not do what you will regret; and if you do,
Do not regret.*

656.

Do not do what the wise condemn
Even to save your starving mother.

657.

Better the poverty of the wise
Than wealth got with infamy.

658.

Those who do what is forbidden
May get their ends but will come to grief.

659.

Goods gained with others' tears are lost with one's own:
Well-got, even when lost, help hereafter.

660.

To stock ill-got wealth is to store
Water in unburnt clay.

67. Efficiency

661.

Efficiency is but strength of mind:
All aids mere aids.

662.

To shun ruin, and ruined not give up
Are the two rules the wise prescribe.*

663.

Let ends reveal deeds: a hand disclosed
Breeds endless woe.

664.

It is easy for anyone to talk,
But hard to act thereon.

665.

Efficient deeds inspired by fame
Redound to the king and win esteem.

666.

All one aims at can be gained
If one is but firm.

667.

Don't despise by looks: the linchpin holds
The huge wheel in place.

668.

Decide clear-eyed and act firmly
Without delay.

669.

However great the hardship,
Pursue with firmness the happy end.

670.

The world has no use for those however strong
Who have no use for firmness.

68. Modes of Action

671.

The end of deliberation is decision:
To decide and dawdle is bad.

672.

Delay where delay is needed, but do not delay
When you must act.

673.

Strike where possible; elsewhere
Consider other means.

674.

Aggression or enmity left half-way
Is fire half put out.

675.

Five things should be pondered over before you act:
Resources, weapons, time, place and deed.*

676.

Weigh well before you plunge
The inputs, impediments and gain.

677.

The way to do a thing is to get
Inside an insider.

678.

Let one action get another
As an elephant an elephant.

679.

More urgent than helping friends
Is making friends with the enemy's foes.*

680.

If you are weak and fear internal trouble
Seize conciliation.

69. Envoys

681.

Amiability, breeding and ways that attract kings
Are essential in an envoy.

682.

An envoy's three essentials
Are loyalty, intelligence and sagacious speech.

683.

An envoy should be expert in knowledge
To succeed with the powerful.

684.

Let him go as envoy who has sense,
Personality and scholarship.

685.

An envoy's words should be compact, unoffending,
Pleasant and useful.

686.

An envoy should be well-read, not nervous,
Persuasive and resourceful.

687.

It is best to know one's job, time and place,
And rehearse one's words.*

688.

Morality, sociability, courage and truth
Should characterize a messenger.

689.

A king's herald will not even negligently
Utter words that leave a stain.

690.

A good envoy will maintain his king's good
Even risking boldly his own life.

70. To Move with Kings

691.

Courtiers round a king, like men before a fire,
Should be neither too far nor too near.

692.

The way to gain gifts from a king
Is not to covet what he covets.

693.

Beware and ward off faults—suspicion roused
Is hard to clear.

694.

Avoid before the great
Whispers and knowing smiles.

695.

Neither eavesdrop nor pursue a king's secret—
Wait till he tells himself.

696.

Speak to him shunning the unpleasant
And according to his mood, time and likes.

697.

Tell the useful and even when asked
Avoid always the useless.

698.

Don't treat him lightly as young or kin
But act as befits his splendour.

699.

The level-headed do not presume on esteem
And do wrong.

700.

To presume on an old friendship and do wrong
Is to court disaster.

71. Mind Reading

701.
He is a jewel on this sea-girt earth
Who can read a thought without being told.

702.
The sure apprehension of another mind
Is the mark of a god.*

703.
He is worth any price who by intuition
Can read another's thought.

704.
Only in their limbs do other men resemble
A thought reader.

705.
What use are eyes that cannot read
A man's thoughts on his face?

706.
As a mirror shows what is in front
So the face reveals the full mind.

707.
What is as informed as the face
The index in front of joy and sorrow?

708.
Just stand and look before a feeling heart
To have your woes redressed.

709.
The eyes will reveal to those that can read them
Both love and hate.

710.
The astute, you will find, use for their gauge
Nothing but eyes.

72. Knowing an Assembly

711.

Meticulous masters of words
Must suit them carefully to the council.

712.

Orators who wish to do good
Should study the occasion with care.

713.

Those are poor orators, unavailing,
Who speak without knowing their audience.

714.

Sparkle mid the sparkling, and be chalk-white,
Among the blank.

715.

The best of virtues is the modesty
Which holds back before seniors.

716.

A slip in a learned assembly
Is like sliding at the gate to heaven.*

717.

Scholarship shines in an assembly
Of meticulous scholars.

718.

Speaking before those quick to grasp
Is watering a plant in fertile soil.

719.

Don't tell an assembly of fools even forgetfully
Things meant for wise men.

720.

To address an unfit audience
Is to spill nectar in a sewer.

73. Facing an Assembly

721.

The expert speaker will make no slip
Addressing an assembly he has gauged.

722.

Most learned among the learned is he
Whose learning the learned accept.

723.

Many face death in battle: only a few
Face an assembly.

724.

Let the learned learn from you, and you
From one more learned.

725.

Learn grammar and dialectics that you may
Be fearless in dispute.

726.

What use is a sword to a coward
Or learning to the tongue-tied?

727.

The learning of the tongue-tied
Is a sword in a poltroon's hand.*

728.

They are useless however learned
Who cannot impress the wise.

729.

The world will rate the tongue-tied scholar
As worse than the ignorant.

730.

Those who through stage-fright keep their learning to themselves
Though living, are dead.

74. The Land

731.

Tireless farmers, learned men and honest traders
Constitute a country.

732.

Wealth large and enviable, and produce free of pests
Make up a country.

733.

The hallmark of an ideal land
Is to bear all burdens and pay all taxes willingly.

734.

An ideal land is free of hunger,
Pestilence and war.

735.

Groupism, internal dissensions and seditious chiefs
Are absent in an ideal land.

736.

That land is called leading which knows no evil days
And whose yields can meet bad days when they come.

737.

A land's limbs are water of two kinds,* hills with streams well-
placed
And a strong fortress.

738.

Health, wealth, fertility, joy and safety
Are called a land's five ornaments.

739.

Call that a land which yields without toil,
Not that where toil precedes yield.

740.

All excellences are vain
Where ruler and ruled disagree.

75. Forts

741.
A fort is paramount
Alike to aggressor and defender.

742.
Blue water, open space, hills and thick forests
Constitute a fortress.

743.
The books prescribe that fortress walls
Should be high, thick, strong and impregnable.

744.
A fortress spacious with few weak spots
Will demoralize a foe.

745.
A good fortress is hard to seize, well-supplied
And suited to those within.

746.
With all things needed a fort should have
An efficient garrison.

747.
No siege, storm or treachery
Can take a good fort.

748.
In a good fort, the besieged
Can withstand and defeat the foe.

749.
A good fort gains fame
Frustrating its siege at the outset.

750.
A fortress however good is nothing
Without men mighty in action.

76. Wealth

751.

There is nothing like wealth
To make the worthless worthy.

752.

Everyone despises the poor
And extol the rich.

753.

Wealth, a lamp never going out,
Dispels the gloom in distant lands.

754.

Wealth acquired sinless and well
Yields both virtue and happiness.

755.

Wealth unblessed by giver and taker
Should not be touched.

756.

Ownerless property, tools and tributes
Belong to the king.

757.

Compassion child of love, is nourished
By wealth, the generous foster-mother.

758.

A wealthy man's undertakings
Are elephant fights witnessed from a hill.

759.

Stock wealth: no steel sharper than that
To cut down your foe's pride.

760.

Shining wealth well-gathered
Attracts the other two.*

77. Army

761.

The greatest wealth of a king is an army
Well-manned and fearless.

762.

Veterans alone stand firm in dire straits
Decimated but fearless.

763.

An army of rats may roar like the sea,*
But the hiss of a cobra will silence it.

764.

Tried soldiers who cannot be bought
Are an army's best part.

765.

That is an army which stands together
And defies death itself.

766.

Courage, honour, tradition and steadfastness
Are an army's four shields.

767.

An army should withstand and confound
The foe's tactics, and advance.

768.

An army poor in advance and defence
May yet make a big show.

769.

An army will win where there is no desertion,
Disaffection and niggardliness.

770.

However many and good its soldiers
An army without leaders will melt away.

78. Valour

771.

"Foes, don't withstand my chief—many who did
Now stand as stone!"*

772.

Better the spear that missed an elephant
Than the arrow that killed a hare.

773.

Valour in battle is called manliness,
But help in a foe's distress cuts deeper.

774.

Losing his spear hurled at a tusker
A hero grabs happily the one skewering him.*

775.

When a foe hurls his spear, even to wink
Is to a hero retreat.

776.

Days devoid of honourable wounds
Are to a hero a waste.

777.

That hero is worthy of his anklet*
Who gives up his life for fame.

778.

Even a king's wrath cannot hold back
Heroes ready to die in battle.

779.

Who dares despise a man for not fulfilling
A pledge he died to fulfil?

780.

How welcome is the death which brings
Tears to a grateful king!

79. Friendship

781.

What is rarer to get than friendship
And a stronger shield against a foe?

782.

Wise men's friendship waxes like the crescent
And fools', like the full moon, wanes.

783.

Good friends are like good books—
A perpetual delight.

784.

Friendship is not for jollity
But swift correction when needed.

785.

Friendship needs neither touch nor time
But like feelings alone.

786.

One may smile and smile and be no friend
The heart should smile with the face.

787.

Friendship curbs wrong, guides right,
And shares distress.

788.

Swift as one's hand to slipping clothes
Is a friend in need.

789.

Friendship reigns there where, ever the same,
It gives every help.

790.

That friendship is mean which boasts,
"He loves me and I him".

80. Choosing Friends

791.
There is nothing worse than rash friendship
For friends once made can't be abandoned.

792.
Make friends in haste
And repent at leisure.

793.
Make one a friend after knowing
His nature, family, fellows and flaws.

794.
A man of birth and scrupulous honour
Is worth seeking even at a price.

795.
Seek a friend who will make you cry,
Rail and rate when you go astray.

796.
Adversity has this use—as a yardstick
To spread out and measure friends.*

797.
It is a godsend to be rid
Of friendship with fools.

798.
Avoid diffidence
And deserters in need.

799.
A friend's betrayal rankles
Even on the deathbed.

800.
Seek the friendship of the pure, and shake off
The worthless even at a price.

81. Old Friends

801.

Call that an old friendship
Where liberties are not resented.

802.

The soul of friendship is freedom
Which the wise should welcome.

803.

What is that intimacy which does not approve
And reciprocate liberties?

804.

The wise are pleased when friends take the liberty
Of doing what *they* should have done.

805.

If friends hurt, put it down
To ignorance or familiarity.

806.

True friends* will not give up old comrades
Even when they have brought harm.

807.

Old friends won't cease to love
Even when injured.

808.

The friend who will not hear his friend decried
Hails the day his friend offends.

809.

The world loves him who sticks
To a long friendship.

810.

Even foes love those who are loyal
To an erring friend.

82. Bad Friends

811.

The love of the worthless however ardent
Had better decrease than grow.

812.

What matter if one gain or lose
A motivated friendship?

813.

Designing friends are no better
Than prostitutes and thieves.

814.

Better no friends than those who resemble
Horses unbroken on the battlefield.

815.

Better no friends than the base
Who betray at need.

816.

A wise man's enmity is a crore of times better
Than a fool's fast friendship.

817.

Ten crore times better the enmity of foes
Than the friendship of jesters and fools.

818.

Drop silently the friends who pose
And won't help when they can.

819.

Friends whose words differ from their deeds
Distress even in dreams.

820.

Keep them far off who are friends at home
And foes in public.

83. False Friends

821.
False friends are anvils, not aids
When you are struck.*

822.
Fickle as a woman's heart
Is feigned friendship.

823.
Hateful enmity is not affected
By wide learning.

824.
Beware of those who smile without
And are false within.

825.
When minds do not agree
Don't trust mere words.

826.
A foe's words though seeming friendly
Can be read at once.

827.
Don't trust the bowing speech of a foe
Any more than a bow.

828.
Folded hands may conceal a dagger—
Likewise a foe's tears.

829.
It is politics to please and hoodwink those
Who flatter but despise us.

830.
When the foe approaches like a friend
Smile, but don't befriend.

84. Folly

831.

Folly lies in seizing what brings ill
And letting the good slip.

832.

The folly of follies is to love
The improper.

833.

A fool has no sense of shame, or curiosity,
Or love, or regard.

834.

There is no greater fool than he
Who has studied and taught, but lacks control.

835.

A fool does deeds in a single birth
That will plunge him in hell in the succeeding seven.

836.

When a fool takes on a task,
The task is undone, and so is he!

837.

When a fool gets a fortune, his nearest starve
And strangers are sated.

838.

A fool getting hold of wealth
Is like a lunatic getting drunk.

839.

Sweet indeed is a fool's friendship—
For when it breaks there is no pain.

840.

A fool's entry into a learned assembly
Is like a dirty foot on a clean bed.*

85. Conceit

841.

The lack of lacks is the lack of knowledge—
Other lacks are not deemed such by the world.

842.

If one gets a gift from a fool
It is just a piece of luck.

843.

The harm fools do to themselves
Is beyond anything their foes do to them.

844.

Folly is nothing but the conceit
That one is wise.

845.

Pretence to learning not learnt
Calls in question the learning learnt.

846.

Can a fool be said to be clothed
When his faults lie exposed?

847.

A fool's greatest harm to himself
Is rejecting precious knowledge.*

848.

A fool who neither knows nor listens to others
Is a plague till he dies.

849.

He is blind who would make the blind see
Who can only see as they used to.

850.

He who denies what the world affirms
Will be thought a demon.

86. Malice

851.

Malice, they say, is the disease
Which breeds aversion to all life.

852.

Even if another's hatred causes harm
Avoid hostility and retaliation.

853.

He will achieve undying fame
Who discards hatred.

854.

When the misery of miseries, malice, ceases
Comes the joy of joys.

855.

Who would want to fight against him
That has no hatred in his heart?

856.

A man fond of hostility
Will lose quickly wealth and life.

857.

Those rapt up in destructive hate
Will never see the great truths in moral codes.

858.

To resist hatred is a gain,
To yield to it ruin.

859.

Destined to prosper one will not look at hatred;
Destined for ruin, will see it all the time.

860.

From hatred comes all evil; and from love
The riches of virtue.

87. Easy Targets

861.
Avoid warfare with the strong,
And choose the weak for foes.

862.
Loveless, without support and weak,
How can one withstand attack?

863.
A coward, ignorant, unsocial and mean
Is an easy prey to his enemy.

864.
The unrestrained and angry are an easy prey
To anyone, anytime, anywhere.

865.
An erring, remiss, shameless cad
Is welcome to his foes.

866.
Blind fury and inordinate lust
Are easy targets.

867.
He is a foe worth purchasing
Who starts a fight and does all wrong.

868.
Lacking virtue and full of faults
The friendless strengthen the enemy.

869.
His joy is immense who gets for his foe
A fool and a coward.

870.
Fame will escape him who lets escape
An easy victory over a fool.

88. Strategy

871.

War is an evil which none even in jest
Should desire.

872.

Make foes of bowmen if you must,
Never of penmen.

873.

More destitute than a lunatic is the lone fighter
With multiple foes.

874.

The world is secure under one whose nature
Can make friends of foes.

875.

Facing two foes, unaided and alone
Make one your friend.

876.

When hard beset keep your options open
Even among those previously tested.

877.

Keep your sorrows from your friends
And your weakness from your foes.

878.

Plan, strengthen and guard yourself,
And your foe's hopes will collapse.

879.

Cut a thorn betimes—grown a tree
It will hurt the hand that cuts.

880.

The foe despised and not put down;
May blast you with a breath.

89. The Enemy Within

881.

Even shade and water not wholesome will harm—
Likewise one's kinsmen.

882.

No need to fear the enemy with swords—
Beware of the false friend.

883.

Beware of the foe within—like the potter's knife
He might cut you at the nick.

884.

Lying dissensions breed many evils
That break up unity.

885.

Secret dissensions caused by kinsmen
May lead to disaster and death.

886.

A break where there should be unity
Is no way to avoid death.

887.

A house divided like a vial and its lid
Seems one but comes apart.*

888.

A house with internal foes will wear out
Like iron filed.

889.

Internal dissension is a small seed
That harbours a huge growth.

890.

To partner one with a hidden hate
Is to share a hut with a cobra.

90. Irreverence

891.

The best way to guard oneself
Is not to slight the powerful.

892.

Irreverence to the great will lead
To endless trouble through them.

893.

To offend the powerful wantonly
Is to ask for trouble.

894.

For the weak to challenge the mighty
Is for a mortal to beckon death.

895.

Where can he find shelter and escape
Who falls foul of a powerful king?

896.

One may survive a fire but not the ire
Of a sage offended.

897.

What avails pomp and wealth if one
Rouses the wrath of a sage?

898.

If the rock-like sages wish to destroy
Those seeming rooted will perish utterly.

899.

Even kings will collapse
If a sage's wrath is roused.

900.

Kings with all their army and kin
Cannot survive a sage's wrath.

91. Uxoriousness

901.

Wives unduly exalted impede
Virtue and career.

902.

The unmanly doings of an uxorious man
Are a public scandal.

903.

Cowardly submission to one's wife leads
To endless shame among decent men.

904.

A henpecked husband acquires no virtue,
Nor do his deeds achieve fame.

905.

A man who fears his wife will always fear
To do good to the good.

906.

Those who fear their wives' slender shoulders
May live like gods but are not men.

907.

Better a shy woman herself than the effeminate man
Who does a woman's bidding.

908.

A doting husband will have no time
For friends or virtuous deeds.

909.

Virtue, wealth and happiness
Are not for the henpecked.

910.

The firm-willed are forever free
Of uxorious folly.

92. Public Women

911.

Fraught with ill are the sweet words
Of jewelled women who sell their love.

912.

See through and avoid the immoral women
Who talk of morals with a purpose.

913.

A harlot's embrace feigning love for lucre
Is like one clasping an alien corpse in a dark room for money.*

914.

The wise seeking grace will have no use
For prostitutes seeking mammon.

915.

Men of wisdom inborn or acquired
Will find no joy in the cheap delight of a harlot.

916.

Those who would spread their good name will not touch
Others who spread their charms for money.

917.

The empty-hearted alone will embrace
Hearts that go not with their bodies.

918.

A false woman's embrace is a siren's
To one who cannot see through it.

919.

The soft shoulders of those who sell their charms
Are a bog for low minds.

920.

Fortune leaves those whose friends
Are wantons, wine and dice.

93. Abstinence

921.

A wine-lover strikes no fear in his foes
And his glory wanes.

922.

Drink no wine, or let them drink it
Who do not care what wise men think.

923.

When a drunkard's glee hurts his own mother,
Why speak of the wise?

924.

The good lady Shame averts her face
From the disgusting vice of drunkenness.

925.

Rank ignorance alone will pay for and get
Self-ignorance.

926.

The sleeping do not differ from the dead—
Nor wine from poison.

927.

The secret drinker with his drooping eyes
Is the village butt.

928.

Don't say, "I never drank":
Secrets will be out when drunk.

929.

As well search for a drowned man with a lamp under water
As reason with one drowned in drink.

930.

When a drunkard sober sees another drunk
Why does he not note his own damage?

94. Gambling

931.

Don't gamble even if you win—
Your gain is a bait to draw you in.

932.

Can gamblers ever thrive
Who gain one and lose a hundred?

933.

To be lost all the time in the rolling dice
Is to lose your wealth to others.

934.

There is nothing like gambling to bring
Poverty, sorrow and disgrace.

935.

They lose all who will not give up
The dice, the board and the throw.

936.

Those caught by the Goddess of Poverty called Dice
Will starve on earth and burn in hell.*

937.

Time wasted in a gambling house
Loses ancestral wealth and worth.

938.

Dicing loses wealth, imposes lies,
Kills grace and causes sorrow.

939.

The gambler will lose riches and renown,
Learning, food and clothes.

940.

Life goes on in spite of sorrow
And stakes in spite of loss!

95. Medicine

941.

Three things beginning with wind, say the experts,
In excess or lacking cause disease.*

942.

His body needs no drugs who only eats
After digesting what he ate before.

943.

Past food digested, eat in measure
And so live long.

944.

Assured of digestion and truly hungry
Eat with care agreeable food.

945.

Agreeable food in moderation
Ensures absence of pain.

946.

As health to a moderate eater
So disease sticks to a glutton.

947.

Measureless eating the stomach cannot tackle
Causes measureless ills.

948.

Diagnose with care, discover the cause,
And find and apply the remedy.

949.

A doctor should treat taking account
Of the patient, the illness and the time.

950.

The patient, the doctor, the remedy and attendant
Are medicine's four limbs.

(iii) Miscellaneous

96. Lineage

951.
Integrity and shame are natural
Only to the well-born.

952.
Men of birth will never slip
In conduct, truth and refinement.

953.
A smiling face, a generous heart, sweet words and no scorn
Are said to mark the well-born.

954.
Men of birth will not be mean
Even for countless wealth.

955.
An ancient family may default in charity,
Never in their conduct.

956.
Those wedded to their spotless heritage
Will do nothing unworthy or false.

957.
A failing in a noble family
Stands out like the moon's spot.

958.
His lineage is suspect
Who is harsh and loveless.

959.
The plant betrays the soil, and his speech
The man of birth.

960.
There is no good without a sense of shame
Nor high birth without politeness.

97. Honour

961.

Reject base actions even if such rejection
Makes life impossible.

962.

Those who desire fame with honour
Will not sacrifice honour for fame.

963.

In prosperity, bend low;
In adversity, stand straight.

964.

Men fallen from high estate
Are like hair fallen from the head.

965.

Even a hill-like eminence can be brought low
By a small speck.

966.

Why pursue the proud and get
No name on earth, no place in heaven?

967.

Rather than the life of a dependant
Prefer death on the spot.

968.

Does life saved at the cost of honour
Put death off forever?

969.

Like the yak that dies for its hair
Some die for their honour.

970.

The world sings the praise of those who prefer
Death to dishonour.

98. Greatness

971.

Glory is the desire to excel;
And to live without it, shame.

972.

Birth is alike to all—but not their worth
Because of their diverse deeds.

973.

The high who act low are not high,
Nor the low who act high, low.

974.

Fame is a jealous mistress
And will brook no rival.

975.

The great will achieve deeds
Rare in achievement.

976.

The small are incapable of regard
For the great.

977.

The good points of the small-minded
Only make them arrogant.

978.

The great are always humble, and the small
Lost in self-admiration.

979.

Greatness is never puffed up, while the small
Are inordinately proud.

980.

The great hide others' faults—
Only the small talk of nothing else.

99. Character

981.

All virtues are said to be natural to those
Who acquire character as a duty.

982.

To the wise the only worth
Is character, naught else.

983.

The pillars of excellence are five—love, modesty,
Altruism, compassion, truthfulness.

984.

The core of penance is not killing,
Of goodness not speaking slander.

985.

The secret of success is humility;
It is also wisdom's weapon against foes.

986.

The touchstone of goodness is to own one's defeat
Even to inferiors.

987.

What good is that good which does not return
Good for evil?

988.

Poverty is no disgrace.
To one with strength of character.

989.

Seas may whelm, but men of character
Will stand like the shore.

990.

If the great fail in nobility, the earth
Will bear us no more.

100. Courtesy

991.

Accessibility, they say, is the easy way
To be courteous to all.

992.

Gentle kin and kindliness combined
Constitute courtesy.

993.

Not with their bodies do people come together
But with their gifts and graces.

994.

The world loves the gentility which combines
Justice with benevolence.

995.

Mockery hurts even in jest, and hence
The kindly are courteous even to their foes.

996.

The world goes on because of good men—
Else it will turn to dust.

997.

Their minds may be sharp as files, but the boorish
Behave like trees.

998.

It is base to be discourteous
Even to one's enemies.

999.

This world is dark even at noon
To those who cannot laugh.

1000.

A boor's great wealth is milk gone sour
In a can unscrubbed.

101. Useless Wealth

1001.

A miser makes of his vast wealth
No more use than a corpse.

1002.

The hoarder deluded that wealth was all
Haunts it as a ghost when dead.

1003.

They are a burden on earth who prefer
Hoarding to fame.

1004.

What does he think will survive him
Whom none loves?

1005.

He is poor though a millionaire
Who neither gives nor spends.

1006.

Riches are a curse when neither enjoyed
Nor given to the worthy.

1007.

Wealth not given to the needy
Like a lovely spinster goes to waste.

1008.

The wealth of the unloved
Is a poison tree which ripens at hand.

1009.

Strangers shall possess that wealth
Amassed without love, comfort or scruples.

1010.

The poverty of the virtuous will pass
Like drought before rain.

102. Nicety

1011.

Girls are shy by nature: real shyness
Refrains from a mean act.

1012.

Food, clothes and the rest are common to all—
Distinction comes with nicety.

1013.

All life is attached to the body,
All excellence to nicety.

1014.

Isn't nicety the jewel of the great
And, the lack of it pomposity and a curse?

1015.

The world regards him as nicety's abode
To whom another's shame is his own.

1016.

Noble men will not accept the world itself
Unfenced by nicety.

1017.

Those attached to nicety will lose their life for it,
Never nicety for their life.

1018.

Virtue will shrink from one who does not shrink
From what others shrink from.

1019.

Bad conduct loses caste, but all is lost
By lack of shame.

1020.

Those not controlled by innate nicety
Are puppets miming life, controlled by a string.

103. Social Service

1021.

There is nothing more glorious than to persist
In the advance of the community.*

1022.

Ceaseless zeal and wisdom—these two—
Advance the community.

1023.

Fate itself girds up its loins and rushes
To help one bent on social service.

1024.

Success will come of itself
To the hard social worker.

1025.

The world will flock round one devoted
To honest social service.

1026.

True manliness is the taking on
Of the leadership of one's people.

1027.

In social work as in the battlefield
The burden falls on the fit.

1028.

There is no set time for social service:
To put off and be finical is ruinous.

1029.

"Must my body be a cup of bitterness?"
Might well be the reformer's cry.

1030.

Society will crash axed by misfortune
Without good men to support it.

104. Agriculture

1031.

After trying other jobs the world comes to the plough,
Which though hard is best.

1032.

Ploughmen are the earth's axle-pin;
They carry all the world.

1033.

They only live whose food is what they raise—
The rest must cringe and trail.

1034.

The might of many kingdoms comes under the shade
Of the ploughman's full-eared corn.

1035.

Those who eat what their hands produce
Neither beg nor refuse a beggar.

1036.

If ploughmen fold their hands
There is neither food nor penance.

1037.

If the ploughed soil dries to a fourth
A fat crop follows without manure.

1038.

Manure more than plough, and after weeding
Guard more than water.

1039.

A negligent husbandman reaps no more joy
Than a neglectful husband.

1040.

The good earth laughs at those who sit back and say,
"We are poor".

105. Poverty

1041.
There is nothing like poverty
But poverty.

1042.
The villain Poverty makes impossible
Both joy on earth and salvation in heaven.

1043.
Craving, the child of Poverty, kills at once
Ancestral pride and gentle speech.

1044.
Poverty will induce dejection and whining
Even in the well-born.

1045.
The misery of poverty attracts and includes
Various miseries.

1046.
A poor man's words however well-informed
Carry no weight.

1047.
Even his mother looks askance
At one cursed with want.

1048.
"Will that hunger come again", wails poverty,
"Which almost killed me yesterday?"

1049.
One may sleep through fire, but the needy
Cannot close his eyes.

1050.
The destitute who will not die themselves
Are a death to others' soup and salt.*

106. Begging

1051.

Beg of the worthy—if they refuse,
The fault is theirs, not yours.

1052.

Begging is a pleasure if what is asked
Comes without pain.

1053.

There is beauty even in begging
Of an honest and virtuous man.

1054.

Of one who will not deny even in his dream
Begging is like granting.

1055.

Men stand expectant only because the world
Has a few who won't refuse.

1056.

Where the illness of refusal is absent
All ills of penury disappear.

1057.

The glad heart rejoices within when it sees
One who gives without scorn.

1058.

Without charity this beautiful world
Becomes a stage for puppets.

1059.

What fame will givers achieve
But for beggars?

1060.

The denied suppliant should not chafe—
His own want proves Fortune's fickleness.

107. The Dread of Begging

1061.
Better a crore of times not beg
Even of dear ones eager to give.

1062.
If some must beg and live, let the Creator
Himself beg and die!

1063.
No greater folly than the hope
That begging will rid poverty.

1064.
More than all the world is his
Who has nothing but won't beg.

1065.
There is nothing sweeter than even the watery gruel
Earned by one's own thews.

1066.
No greater disgrace for the tongue than to beg
Even if only water for a cow.

1067.
Of all those who beg, *I* would beg,
"Beg, if you must, but not of a niggard".

1068.
Begging, that cheat of a raft, will be wrecked
By the rock of refusal.

1069.
The heart melts at the thought of begging
And dies at the thought of denial.

1070.
What does that word do to the refuser
Which kills the suppliant?

108. The Base

1071.

We have not found such another simulacrum
As the mean who look like men.

1072.

More blessed than the good are the base—
For they have no scruples.

1073.

The base are like the gods: they also do
Whatever they like.

1074.

The base are proud when they find
Men meaner than themselves.

1075.

Fear is the base man's only code—
And, on occasion, greed.

1076.

The base are like a drum with which
No secret is safe.

1077.

The base will give to a clenched fist only,
Never out of charity.

1078.

A word will move the noble, while the base
Like sugarcane must be crushed.

1079.

The base excel in slandering those
Whose affluence they can't bear.

1080.

What use are the base in a crisis
Save to rush and sell themselves?

Book III

LOVE

(i) Furtive Love

109. Fascination

1081.
"A goddess? Or a rare peacock? Or a woman
Decked with jewels?" asks my heart amazed.

1082.
Giving look for look, the fair one
Brings an army with her.

1083.
I never saw Death before, and now I see
That it is warring eyes in a woman's form.

1084.
Don't eyes that kill all those they lookup on
Ill-beseem a woman?

1085.
Is it Death, or eyes, or an antelope?
This woman's looks recall all three.

1086.
If my brows were but straight and intervened
Her eyes wouldn't make mine tremble.

1087.
Like the face-cover on a wild elephant
Is the cloth on her swelling breasts!

1088.
How has my might, fearful in the field,
Fallen, brow-beaten!

1089.
What need of outward jewels has she
Doe-eyed, and decked with modesty?

1090.
Wine won't delight unless imbibed
But love with a look delights!

110. Hints

1091.

Her greedy eyes have a double role—
They kill and cure.

1092.

Her stealthy glance is more than half
Love's embrace.

1093.

She looked, and dropped her head, and so
Watered the plant of love.

1094.

When I look, she bends her eyes:
When *I* don't, *she* looks and smiles!

1095.

She didn't stare at me, but smiled
And seemed to wink.

1096.

Where words are curt, but not the heart,
A wink is as good as a nod.

1097.

Words which are bitter, and looks which feign ire
Only mark the seeming-indifferent.

1098.

Her pitying smile to my pleading look
Hinted happiness.

1099.

To look at each other as if they were strangers
Belongs to lovers alone.

1100.

When eyes with eyes commingle
What do words avail?

111. The Joys of Embracing

1101.
In her alone, my jewel, can I find
The joys of sight, smell, hearing, taste and touch.

1102.
Medicines differ from ills, their enemies;
But this my jewel is both disease and cure.

1103.
Can even the Lotus-eyed's heaven give the rest
I find in my love's soft shoulders?*

1104.
Whence did she get the fire which burns when far,
And cools when near?

1105.
Instant and unfailing the joy
My beloved flower-decked gives.

1106.
Her shoulders must be nectar—
They revive me when I droop.

1107.
Clasping this girl my joy is already
A householder's who works, shares and eats.*

1108.
Sweet indeed is that embrace wherein
Not a breath comes between.

1109.
To fall out, make up, and embrace again
Are the fruits of love fulfilled.

1110.
Exploring this girl I know
That love, like learning, never ends.

112. In Praise of his Lady

1111.

Hail, *aniccham*, tender flower!
But more tender is my love.

1112.

My heart, how deluded you are
To match her eyes with common flowers!

1113.

Her body is a shimmer, smile pearls, scent fragrance, .
Eyes spears and shoulders bamboos.

1114.

Seeing her the *kuvalai** hangs its head
Unable to rival her eyes.

1115.

She wore the *aniccham*, stalk and all—
Her waist will break, its knell tolled!*

1116.

The stars roam perplexed
Not able to tell the moon from my love.

1117.

Is there a spot on my love's face
As on the inconstant moon?

1118.

O moon, if you could shine like my love,
You too I shall love.

1119.

O moon, if you would imitate my darling,
Cease to be common.

1120.

The *aniccham* and the swan's down
Are spikes to my love's sole.

113. In Praise of the Beloved

HE

1121.

My love's white teeth and soft lips
Are milk and honey.

1122.

As life to body, is the bond
Between me and this maid.

1123.

Depart, the idol in my eye,
That my love may enter.

1124.

Embracing my love is life,
Separation from her death.

1125.

I can't *recall* her bright eyes—
We recall only the forgotten!

SHE

1126.

He is always before me, even when I wink
Invisible to others.

1127.

I will not paint my eyes and so lose
Even for a trice the sight of my love.

1128.

I dare not swallow anything hot
Lest it hurt my lover within me!

1129.

I never close my eyes lest he escape—
And they call *him* heartless!*

1130.

He dwells gladly forever in my heart—
And they say he is loveless and has left me.

114. Unabashed

1131.

To know love and to lose it! No way but this—
To mount the *madal* to have it again.*

1132.

Away with shame! Soul and body
Can bear no more, and will mount the *madal*.

1133.

I *had* manliness once and shame, but today
Wish only to mount the *madal*.

1134.

What is the raft of "Will" and "Won't"
Against love's raging waters?

1135.

Night's yearnings and the *madal* to cure them
Are the gifts of that braceleted girl.

1136.

Even at midnight I think of the *madal*
Sleepless for love of her.

1137.

Women are lucky—their love may rage,
But not for them the *madal*.

SIIE

1138.

Love, pitiless and fearless, has dragged
All my secrets out.

1139.

My love saying, "No one knows me"
Has budded and blown in the streets!

1140.

Fools mock us to our face, not having endured
What we have.*

115. Rumours

1141.

Rumours revive hope—those that spread them
Luckily don't know this.

1142.

Thanks to these people's senseless talk
My darling is now mine.

1143.

Should I not welcome their rumours
That have made possible what lay beyond?

1144.

Rumour has bloated my love which but for it
Might have shrunk.

1145.

As with each draught grows the drinker's delight
So with each talk of love.

SHE

1146.

An eclipse is much noised however brief—
So my one day's meeting with my lover.

1147.

The village gossip manures my love,
And my mother's reproaches water it.

1148.

To suppress love with scandal
Is to put fire out with *ghee*!

1149.

"I'll never leave you", he said, and left:
So shamed, why shun rumours?

1150.

This village talk is what we wanted—
It is now up to my lover.

(ii) Wedded Love

116. Separation

1151.

Tell me if he is *not* going; of his soon return
Tell my survivors.*

1152.

To expect was the joy—the union itself
Foreboding separation was a sorrow.

1153.

How hard it is to trust when even he who knows
Breaks his word and goes!

1154.

Is it the trustful you will blame
Loved, assured and left behind?

1155.

If *me* you would serve, stop *him* going;
Gone we shall not meet again.

1156.

Of one so cruel as to talk of going
It is vain to hope return and love.

1157.

That my lord has left me
My slipping bracelets tell.*

1158.

It is sad to live among strangers,
Bitter to part with one's love.

1159.

Can fire burn like love,
Even untouched?

1160.

Strange how many can bear separation,
Survive sorrow, and live!

117. Pining

1161.

I would hide this sickness gladly,
But it wells up like a spring.

1162.

Hide this sickness I cannot;
To tell him who caused it I am ashamed.

1163.

Love and shame hang poised on my life;
My body unable to bear them.

1164.

I see the sea of love but not the raft
On which to cross it.

1165.

If friendship can work such woe,
What will enmity?

1166.

Love's joy is as the sea,
Its pangs vaster.

1167.

Caught in love's whirlpool I find no shore;
Darkened I am alone.

1168.

Poor night, putting all things to sleep,
Has only me for company.

1169.

Even more cruel than my cruel lord
Are the long nights now.

1170.

If like my mind my eye could go to him,
It wouldn't be whelmed in a flood of tears.

118. The Eyes' Longing

1171.

Who is to blame? My eyes that caused this fever
Or I powerless to help them?

1172.

Why do these eyes now grieve
That thoughtless had their fill?

1173.

The leaping then and the weeping now
Are laughable.

1174.

They caused me a cureless fever and now
Have wept themselves dry.

1175.

They plunged me in a raging sea of love
And for this must suffer sleepless pain.

1176.

O joy, that the causes of my torment
Are themselves tormented!

1177.

Eyes that so greedily gorged on him,
Weep, weep and dry up!

1178.

He made love with words, not heart; his nearness
Is nothing till I see him.

1179.

Sleepless when he is not here, sleepless when he is,
Either way my eyes never rest.

1180.

If all my secrets are known to the people here,
It's my eye-trumpets you should blame!

119. Pallor

1181.

I agreed to part and so have lost
The right to complain of my pallor.*

1182.

This pallor bestrides me with pride
Because it is his creation.

1183.

He robbed me first of my beauty and shame
And gave in exchange sickness and pallor.

1184.

When my mind and tongue are taken up with him
How does pallor sneak in?

1185.

No sooner is my lord gone
Than pallor comes.

1186.

Darkness lies in wait for the lamp to go out,
And pallor for the embrace to break.

1187.

Locked in embrace I turned a little—
And pallor came in a flood.

1188.

Everyone says, "She is pallid":
No one, "He left her".

1189.

What matters to you, my friend, seems to be
Not my pallor but that *he* shouldn't be blamed!

1190.

If his unkindness is beyond blame
Let *me* be called Pallor personified!

120. The Lonely Anguish

1191.

Theirs is the stoneless fruit of love
Whose love is returned.

1192.

Like the timely rain to the earth
Is the beloved's love to his love.

1193.

The proud boast "We shall live"
Is for those whose love is returned.

1194.

Even those loved are luckless
Unless loved by those *they* love.

1195.

What use is love
Unreturned?

1196.

Love one-sided is bitter,
Balanced, sweet.

1197.

Can't the God of Love, lodged in me alone,
See my pallor and distress?

1198.

Hard is the heart that can survive
Without a word of love.

1199.

Unloved as I am, it is sweet to hear
About my beloved.

1200.

My heart, you tell your anguish to the heartless—
Bless you, go fill the sea!

121. Nostalgia

1201.

Love is sweeter than wine—its mere thought
Intoxicates.

1202.

Love is ever sweet—thought-filled
Parting has no sorrow.

1203.

My sneeze coming up, does not arrive:
So perhaps, my lover's thoughts of me.*

1204.

Do I dwell in his thoughts always
As he in mine?

1205.

Is he not ashamed to keep me out
And come always to me?

1206.

I live always on my past days with him—
What else have I?

1207.

When remembering, my burnt heart hardly lives,
What will happen if I forget?

1208.

However much I think of him, he isn't vexed—
Isn't it great of him?*

1209.

My dear life dies at the thought of his coldness
To whom once we were not two but one.*

1210.

O moon, shine on, so that in you
My eyes meet his, who gone, yet stays.*

122. Love Dreams

1211.

How shall I feast this dream which brought
A message from my lord?

1212.

If my eyes would only close I'll tell my lord
My being's secret at length.

1213.

I live because I see in dreams
The one who scorns me when awake.

1214.

I love dreams because they bring to me
My deserter awake.

1215.

My joy was great then awake
And now too, dreaming.

1216.

Save for that thing called waking
My dream-lover won't leave me indeed.

1217.

Why does he, cruel, torment me in dreams
When he leaves me alone awake?

1218.

Asleep he is round my shoulders,
Awake in my heart again.

1219.

They call him a deserter because
They cannot see him in dreams.

1220.

He is a deserter to these people—
What know they of his dream visits?

123. Evening Sorrows

1221.
Bless you, Evening, no evening
But a bride-killer!

1222.
Bless you, muddled, lack-lustre twilight!
Is your love, too, cruel?

1223.
The evening that once came trembling and pale
Comes now fierce and destructive.

1224.
When my love is away, in strides the evening
Like a murderous foe.

1225.
What good did I do to dawn?
What harm to evening?

1226.
When my love was with me I did not know
How cruel evening could be.

1227.
This my sickness buds in the morning,
Grows through the day, and blossoms at eve.

1228.
The shepherd's pipe, once sweet,
Is the killer evening's harbinger and weapon.

1229.
This place will all be dizzy and grieved
When the evening spreads and smothers me.

1230.
Since wealth is all he cares for, this muddled eve
Will kill my life so long preserved.

124. Wasting Away

1231.

Brooding over him who left us in the dumps
Your eyes now quail before the flowers?

1232.

Dim and tearful, your eyes proclaim
Your lord's cruelty.

1233.

The shoulders that swelled on the bridal day
Now proclaim the parting.

1234.

Your lord away, your thin shoulders droop,
Beauty and bracelets lost.

1235.

Shoulders which droop and bracelets which slip
Proclaim his cruelty.

SHE

1236.

Let drooping shoulders and slipping bracelets be—
I can bear them, but not your censure of him.

1237.

My heart, would you gain glory? Go tell that cruel man
Of the uproar caused by my drooping shoulders.

HE

1238.

Once, when I loosened my embrace,
That poor girl's forehead grew pale.

1239.

Her large eyes dimmed with tears
When but a breath came between us.

1240.

Did those eyes dim in response
To the bright forehead's paling?

125. To her Heart

1241.

My heart, can't you suggest any remedy at all
For this incurable sickness?

1242.

Bless you, my heart: when he does not love us
What folly to pine for him!

1243.

O heart, what use to stay here and pine
When he who causes this sickness is heartless?

1244.

O heart, if you are going to him, take these eyes too;
Else they will eat me up.

1245.

Have we the strength, O heart, to give up one
Who does not love us when we love him?

1246.

O my heart, your wrath is a hoax:
Face to face, you will yield.

1247.

My good heart, give up either love or shame—
Both those *I* cannot bear.

1248.

My heart, you are a fool to chase him
Crying, "He is pitiless"

1249.

Whom are you seeking outside, my heart,
While my dear one is within?

1250.

If I keep the deserter longer in my heart,
My soul too will wither.

126. Farewell, Reserve!

1251.

Love the axe breaks down the bolted door
Of bashful reserve.

1252.

That pitiless thing called Love exploits even at night
Its mother, my heart.*

1253.

Fain would I hide my love, but it breaks out
Like a sneeze.

1254.

I thought I had control, but my love
Breaks all bonds.

1255.

Not for the love-sick is the dignity
That will not chase the indifferent.

1256.

How wonderful is my grief
Seeking the indifferent!

1257.

What do we know of shame when the lover
Does all we long for?*

1258.

Where is that fortress of feminine reserve
That can resist a host of enticing words?

1259.

I said I would hold back, but when my heart went out
I too went with it and clasped him.

1260.

Is it possible for those to freeze
Whose heart melts at a touch?

127. Mutual Longing

SHE

1261.

My fingers are worn marking his absence on the wall,
And my eyes dim looking for him.

1262.

My jewelled friend, if I forget him now
I shall lose for all time both strength and beauty.*

1263.

Courage his mate, he goes courting victory,
While I stay here courting his return.

1264.

The thought of reunion when my love returns
Makes my heart burgeon higher and higher.

1265.

Gorge, eyes, on my love, that the pallor may depart
From my slender shoulders.

1266.

Let my lord return, and one day's draught
Will cure all ills.

1267.

When my darling returns, what shall I do?
Hold back? Go forward? Or both?

HE

1268.

Let the king fight and win; I will tonight
Join my wife, and feast.

1269.

A day is a week to those that yearn
For the far-traveller's return.

1270.

What avail hopes, dreams and the tight embrace
To one dead of a broken heart?

128. Sign Language

HE

1271.

There is something you hide, but your rebellious eyes
Reveal it to me.

1272.

This bamboo-shouldered girl whose beauty fills my eyes
Has too much timidity.

1273.

Her beauty has a thing within
Like the thread in a crystal bead.

1274.

Something lurks behind her smile
Like fragrance in a bud.

1275.

The strategy of that braceleted one
Has a medicine for my ills.

SHE

1276.

This excess of affection and love-making
Perhaps presages their opposite.

1277.

My bangles knew before I did
Of my lord's separation.

1278.

My lord left yesterday, and I have already
A week's pallor.

HER FRIEND TO HIM

1279.

She looked at her bracelets, her slender shoulders
And her feet. That is what she did.*

1280.

A woman is most womanly when herself silent
She makes her eyes declare and plead.

[150]

129. Yearning for Union

1281.

To please with the thought and delight with the sight
Belongs not to liquor but love.

1282.

Where love like a palm fruit is large
A millet of sulks is misplaced.

1283.

Let him neglect me and do what he will—
My eyes will not rest till they see him.

1284.

My friend, I went all set to quarrel—
But my heart forgot and clasped him.

1285.

The eye cannot see the brush which paints it,
Nor I my husband's fault when nighest.

1286.

When I see him I see no faults,
And when I don't, nothing else!

1287.

It is folly to plunge into a raging stream—
Not less to plumb known lies.

1288.

You rogue, your breast, like toddy,
However disgraceful, delights.

1289.

Love is more tender than a flower,
And few there be that feel it.

HE

1290.

Her eyes were resentful, but her clasp
Was tighter than mine.

130. Quarrelling with her Heart

1291.

My heart, you see how his heart is ever his—
Why are you not ever mine?

1292.

My heart, knowing his lack of love
Why do you haunt him in hope?

1293.

Do you now run gladly to him, my heart,
To prove that the ruined have no friends?

1294.

My heart, who will trust you now
When you rush and not sulk before yielding?

1295.

Fear of not getting, and of losing when got—
My heart knows only perpetual fear.

1296.

If my heart stays with me here alone
It is to eat me up.

1297.

My meek and foolish heart will not forget him—
And *I* have forgotten shame!

1298.

My heart fond of life thinks only of him
And pleads that it isn't right to deny him.

1299.

Who will befriend one in sorrow
If not one's own heart?

1300.

When one's own heart behaves like a stranger
Why talk of strangers?

131. Coyness

1301.
Don't yield, sulk let us see a little
His distress.

SHE TO HER

1302.
Love's salt is sulks—a pinch of it welcome,
Too much will ruin the taste.

SHE TO HIM

1303.
To leave a sulky woman alone
Is to add insult to injury.

1304.
To ignore the resentful
Is to cut a fading plant at its root.

HE TO HIMSELF

1305.
The coyness of his delicate darling
Is good even for the good.

1306.
Love without anger and coyness
Is a fruit unripe or rotten.

1307.
Coyness has its drawback—the worry,
How long before union?

1308.
Why grieve when none cares to know
Whether you are grieving?

1309.
Water is sweet in the shade,
And sulks only with one who cares.

1310.
Only my desire makes my heart pine
For union with one who keeps on sulking.

SHE

1311.

Whoremaster, I won't clasp your breast
A common dish for women's eyes to gorge!

1312.

When I sulked, he sneezed; hoping no doubt
I would forget and say "Bless you" *

HE

1313.

If I wear a wreath her blood boils:
"For which woman's sake is this?"

1314.

If I called her "My dearest", she will snap,
"So you have other dears?"

1315.

When I said, "We shouldn't part in this life",
Her eyes filled with tears.*

1316.

"I remembered you". After forgetting?
Said she withdrawing herself!

1317.

"Bless you!" she will say if I sneeze;
Then cry, "Which she is it now?"*

1318.

If I suppress my sneeze, she will say,
"Whom are you wishing to hide?"

1319.

If I plead to make it up with her,
"Aren't you well-practised?"

1320.

If silent I just gaze at her,
She will fume, "Whom are you thinking of?"

133. The Joys of Falling Out

SHE

1321.

He is not to blame, but a little coyness
Will bind him more.

1322.

The pinpricks of sulking do not discourage
But strengthen love.

1323.

Where natures conform like earth and water
Love's quarrels are more than heaven.

1324.

This clinging coyness carries with it
The tool to break down my pride.

HE

1325.

Even for the guiltless it is a joy
To forego briefly love's embrace.

1326.

More than the eating, looking back on it
Gives joy—and so with love.

1327.

In lovers' quarrels the loser wins—
As shown when they make up.

1328.

When shall I know her sulks again
And the ardour which bedewed her brows?

1329.

Sulk, sulk, bright jewel, and let me plead
In endless night!

1330.

The body held back is love's joy,
And the joy of that joy embrace forthcoming!*

NOTES

The number to the left refers to the *Kural* couplet as numbered in the text:

1. A is not only the first letter *a* of Tamil, Sanskrit and other alphabets. Its sound makes possible the pronunciation of the names of all the consonants, e.g., *ka, kha, ga, gha,* etc. God is like *a* in being not only the first, but also the basis, of all creation.

    There is a tradition that Aadi and Bhagavan, the two elements making up the compound word meaning "Primal God" spell respectively the names of Valluvar's mother and father.

2. Professor K. Swaminathan translates *vaalarivan* as "Pure Awareness". "All Indic religions, all sects of Hinduism, Buddhism and Jainism agree on the Supreme Being as one who is Pure, Transcendent non-objective Awareness. This Absolute Awareness is *vaalarivu* which like *maalarivu* whose embodiment is Vishnu is whole and integral. In between we have *paalarivu* (awareness of dualism, male-female, singular-plural) and *nuularivu* (literacy and book-knowledge)".

3. *nilamisai* is literally "on the earth" which is the translation I adopt. Parimeelazhahar, an early and authoritative translator of the *Kural* renders this as "above the earth i.e., in heaven" and most modern translators including F.W. Ellis accept this interpretation.

4. *flower-embedded feet* may refer either specifically to Aruhan the Jain God who is usually represented as standing on a flower, or to God in general whose seat is not only in heaven but also in the flower-shaped-heart of his devotees.

5. Compare Milton's *Lycidas:*

    Fame is no plant that grows on mortal soil...
    But lives and spreads aloft by those pure eyes
    And perfect witness of all-judging Jove.

Not only are bad deeds the result of delusion (success produced by hook or by crook turning to ashes in the mouth), but good deeds too, leading to heaven or rebirth on earth, come in the way of the soul's release.

6. The stanza is almost invariably interpreted as referring not just to anyone who has controlled his senses, but to the Supreme One—God. It may seem strange to refer to God as one who conquered the five senses as if this was for Him a matter of effort. But Mahavira, the founder of Jainism, like the Buddha, took birth as a man and achieved godhead by overcoming the temptations of the flesh.

8. *aravaazhi* could mean either the "ocean of virtue" or the "wheel of virtue", the *dharma chakra*. The latter meaning would be appropriate to the Jain God Aruhan who "caused and possesses the circle of virtue". According to Ellis the dictionaries give the name *antanan* (Brahmin) only to two gods, viz., Brahma (from whom comes Brahmin) and Aruhan. With the meaning "the sea of virtue" the verse could be translated, "Except with that raft, the sea of virtue, other seas cannot be crossed", the other seas being those of wealth and happiness.

9. *engunattaan* could mean either "the one with the most desirable attributes" or "with the eight attributes". Commentators seem to prefer the latter. Parimeelazhahar refers to three such lists, viz., self-existence, pure essence, etc.; the supernatural faculties mentioned in, among other places, the *Amarakosa* (reduction to the least, expansion to the largest, etc.) and infinite wisdom, boundless sight, etc.

17. *tanniirmai kundrum:* A pun seems to be intended on the word *niirmai* which may be derived from *niir* (water) and also means "nature, character". The sea will diminish in the volume of its water, and also be less of itself in its properties, if the cloud absorbing its water does not return it as rain.

23. *irumai vahai terindu:* "knowing the nature of the two". The two could simply be the pleasures of worldliness and the rigours of renunciation. Parimeelazhahar interprets the two as birth

and renunciation. The ascetic chooses the happiness of renunciation in order to avoid the misery of rebirth. At a first glance, the two would seem to be the involvements of worldliness and the freedom of otherworldliness. But Valluvar has the highest praise elsewhere for one who does not avoid the world. The temptation to associate "unreality" and "duplicity" with "the nature of the two" should be resisted, as there is little to suggest that Valluvar is an Advaitin.

25. When Indra, king of heaven, seduced Ahalya, wife of the sage Gautama, the sage cursed him making him both obscene and impotent. The suggestion that it was Indra's conquest over his senses that won him his heavenly kingdom is not convincing.

28. For verbal resemblance, cf., *Tolkaapiyam, Porul*, 480.

29. This is according to Parimeelazhahar's text. An alternative reading *kanamenung* for *kanameyung* will give the meaning "won't hold back even a second".

31. The translation of *sirappu* as release or *moksha* instead of the normal distinction or glory is in accordance with Parimeelazhahar's linking of virtue with the two other *purushaarthas*, viz., wealth and release.

37. Valluvar, like all Hindus, Buddhists and Jains, believed in the doctrine of karma and the working out in successive births the consequences of one's action in a previous birth.

41. "The three other orders": student, *vanaprastha* (forester) and sanyasi. Parallelled by *Manusamhita*, III 77.

42. Parimeelazhahar translates the first word of the couplet not as "ascetics" but as "the abandoned".

43. Cf., *Manusamhita*, III 80-81. The five mentioned there are the *rishis*,.the manes, gods, animals and guests.

49. A simpler rendering than Parimeelazhahar's, "Domestic life is the truly virtuous; that other (viz., renunciation) only if blameless"

58. This accords with Ellis' "Wedded love gives women a foretaste of heaven". Parimeelazhahar interprets this to mean "Women who honour their husbands will be honoured by the gods". Cf., *Manusamhita*, V 155.

61. The literal translation of the heading is "On Begetting Sons", and Parimeelazhahar at any rate, if not Valluvar himself, has a pronounced preference for boys.

62. *All seven births:* These, according to Parimeelazhahar in some of the manuscripts, are plants, reptiles, marine creatures, birds, beasts, humans and gods. They could also be interpreted to mean the seven successive births one may undergo.

63. For the pun on "property" (possession) and "properties" (characteristics) I am indebted to Ellis' rendering of the prose.

64. Cf., *Puranaanuuru*, 188.

68. The verse could also mean "A son surpassing his father in wisdom delights all the world".

73. Since it is not possible to make love without a body, the soul has to be encased in bones. Another interpretation is that the human form is the result of the love a creature bore in its previous manifestations.

74. According to Parimeelazhahar, "The love one bears to one's kindred extends to others and becomes priceless friendship". Or, more succintly, "Love begets desire and that the immeasurable excellence of friendship" (W.H. Drew). But Rajaji's emendation of *nannbu* (friendship) to *nanbu* (enlightenment) seems justified to me in the light of his quotation from Bhuutataazhwaar's *andaadi* stanza I, and I have no hesitation in accepting it.

76. For *vice* Rajaji suggests *valour*. "It also strengthens valour".

85. God will provide for him. Or his hospitality will make him cook the very seed-grains.

90. *aniccam:* an extremely sensitive flower.

101. *Spontaneous aid*: Aid given not as a recompense for previous aid. A variant reading should be translated, "Aid given to those not capable of returning it".

108. Parimeelazhahar interprets *nanru* as "virtue", "virtuous", but the English word "good" is good enough in this context.

111. Justice M.M. Ismail would render this:

> Caught in diversities
> It is good to stick to virtue.

113. According to M.M. Ismail the meaning rather is:

> Avoid at once even the good
> Wrought by evil means.

114. This could refer either to their progeny or to their fame. If to their progeny, either to good and bad children, or to children and no children at all!

126. Cf., *Bhagavad Gita* II 58. The five in the case of the tortoise are his head and four legs, in the man his five senses.

135. Parimeelazhahar cites verse 116 in this connection. But could not the idea be that the envious never feel rich, however rich they may actually be?

154. Ascetics, if they curse when provoked, will lose the fruits of their penance.

167. Lakshmi, the goddess of wealth, rose out of the sea when it was churned. But she was preceded by Muudeevi, the goddess of poverty.

168. The father is the envious man who loses both here and hereafter.

169. The suggestion is that they must be the result of the deeds in a previous birth.

212. An equally valid translation would be:

> Wealth hard-earned is only to help
> The deserving.

220. Such poverty is worth procuring even by selling onself.

223. Or:
> To give before hearing "I lack"
> Is the mark of the well-born.

236. Parimeelazhahar interprets this to mean, "If you are born as a man, have those qualities which will distinguish you from a beast. Failing which, better you were born as a beast".

239. Will become less and less fertile.

255. As he swallows the animals, so hell will swallow him. As once consumed he cannot give them life again, so hell will never give up the sinner which it has swallowed.

256. The meat-eater cannot say that it is the butcher who is responsible for the killing of the birds and the animals that he consumes. Life is made impossible for these creatures because of the meat-eater's appetite for them.

271. *Within:* Both within him (constituting his body) and within themselves (unknown to him).

277. *kunri:* A carob seed, bright red but with a black tip.

295. The Parithiar reading *tanattotu* meaning "better even than a monetary gift" is to be preferred for better rhyme.

306. The Sanskrit for fire is *aasryasan* (the destroyer of the near).

311. "Even for supernal gifts" (Parimeelazhahar).

313. Even righteous indignation is hurtful, to one's self as much as to the provoker! Cf., note to verse 154.

317. *Wilfully hurting:* Manikkudavar's text gives the meaning, "hurting even in thought".

328. Said perhaps with particular reference to animal sacrifices.

336. The usual translation is

> Here yesterday, gone today
> Such greatness is the earth's

but cf., Emerson's "Hamatreya" based on the *Vishnu Purana:* "Earth endures... but where are old men?"

350. Even to God.

354. According to Parimeelazhahar:

> The conquest of the five senses is vain
> Without realization.

365. Renunciation is of the mind, not of the body; of desires, not of material things. The first "free" could also mean "free of future birth".

371. Fated to amass wealth one is energetic, fated to lose it, lazy. But this Fate itself is not a capricious thing but, as Ellis acutely perceives, one's own inescapable past deeds.

391. The second half rendered, "Stop, as beseems", though admissible according to the words and certain philosophies, would contradict note 397 below.

396. Cf., *Manusamhita*, II 218

397. Cf., *Puranaanuuru*, 192 and *Pazhamozhi*, 116.

398. This should be taken in continuation of couplet 397; learning unlike riches accompanies a man from one birth to another.

425. Parimeelazhahar, making no distinction between *odpam* and *arrivu*, interprets the "world" as "the high", "the noble", to whom a wise man should be constant. My interpretation, perhaps a poor one, is my own. It is certainly less forced than Parimeelazhahar's and does not really contradict note 426 below which should be read with my note on it.

426. It is wise, especially for a king, to take into account public opinion and neither ignore nor defy it.

440. Applied to a king, these refer to his amours and the need to guard himself against betrayal to his enemy by keeping him in the dark regarding them.

501. Cf., Kautilya's *Arthasastra*, Book I Chapter 10.

530. This could mean either that he should be cautious against treachery, or that he should investigate whether he had given some cause for the earlier defection which could have been just.

550. Cf., *Manusamhita*, VII 110.

560. Ploughing, weaving, ministering, ruling, trading and teaching. But a better rendering perhaps is "The Brahmins forget their lore".

565. Buried wealth, supposed to be haunted by its dead owner, was not good to him when alive, nor now when he is dead! Cf., 1002.

610. An allusion to one of Vishnu's *avatars* when as Vamana (the Dwarf) he begged of the *asura*, King Bali, for three feet of earth. Having obtained his request he expanded into the huge Trivikrama, measured off the earth with one step, the heavens with another, and for the third foot was offered Bali's head.

617. *Vide* note to 167.

627. To the wise, according to Rajaji, their body is the target of distress; their soul ignores it.

662. "The wise" seems to be mean Sanakya and Kamantaka.

665. This is according to Parimeelazhahar. But according to Dharumar and accepted by Rajaji, the second line should read "Do not repeat it".

675. Cf., Kautilya's *Arthasastra*, Book I Chapter 15.

679. Rajaji however would translate "Make up mis-understandings with your friends in view of the big fight ahead".

687. The translation given here is of the text of Parimeelazhahar, who in his commentary applies this apologetically to an envoy. But Kalingar's text reading *uraipatam tuutu* instead of *uraippaan talai* dispenses with the need for any apology and follows the pattern set by verses 685 and 686, and is also in keeping with verse 690.

702. Cf., *Hamlet:* "In apprehension how like a god!"

716. Cf., Bunyan, *The Pilgrim's Progress*: "There was a way to hell even from the gates of heaven".

727. Literally, a hermaphrodite's.

737. Surface and subsoil.

760. Virtue and happiness. *Vide* 754.

763. *An army of rats:* The word *pakai* meaning "hostility" is almost certainly a mistake for *padai* meaning "an army". The whole chapter deals with army, not like chapter 87 with hostility. Kamban is almost certainly referring to this *kural* when in *Ayodhyakaandam* XII 10 Guha says:

    eli elaam ippadai, aravam yaan

    (To this army of rats I am the serpent.)
    We owe this admirable emendation to M. Shanmukam Pillai.

771. A reference to engravings on, or monuments in stone to commemorate dead warriors.

774. To use an enemy's weapon against him in this fashion seems to have been a common practice.

777. Referring to the ornaments worn traditionally by heroes.

796. "Spread out as in measuring cloth so that defects if any may be disclosed", (Rajaji).

806. *True friends:* Generally rendered, "Friends who stand within the bounds". But would not the meaning rather be, "Those who have savoured the utmost of friendship?"

821. Instead of supporting you, they help in your destruction.

840. A Tamil commentator suggests that more than ordinary dirt is implied here.

847. Or blurting out what should be hidden.

876. The idea is that you never know whose help you may need or who may betray you.

887. "Is like broken copper which cannot be welded", (Rajaji).

913. This could refer to a Nambudri custom mentioned by Abbe Dubois that if amongst them a girl who had attained puberty died unmarried, a man was paid to have a connexion with the corpse, so that the paronts might be exculpated of the sin of not having got her married in time. But that such a custom existed has been denied. In any case it does not obtain any longer.

936. The original Tamil word for gambling was *mukadi*, meaning literally the elder sister. Since the goddess of Poverty is in mythology the elder sister of Lakshmi, the goddess of Fortune, a new name *suudu* was given to gambling so as to avoid an ominous association.

941. Wind, bile and phlegm.

951. To 1080. This section is also called "Lineage" and numbered (iv), (ii) being sections 64–73 "Ministers", and (iii) 74–95 "The Limbs of the State".

1021. The Tamil word *kudi* is generally understood as "family" or "clan" but Rajaji translates it as "community", the social unit in which members participate. This seems to be what Valluvar had in mind. Hence the chapter heading "Social Service".

1050. It is better for them to die than be a burden to others.

1103. Vishnu the second in the Hindu Trinity is always referred to as the "Lotus-eyed".

1107. "Though I have yet to reach that stage by marrying her" is to be understood.

1114. The water-lily.

1115. Even that tender flower will be too much of a burden for her slender waist.

1129. Accusing him as the cause of her sleeplessness.

1131. A lover, driven to proclaiming his love so that he could marry his lover, drew a portrait of her, put down on it her name, the place as well as his own, and mounting a horse made of palm leaves drew it publicly, so that the villagers, the girl's parents or the king might pity him and effect the marriage. This was the ancient practice of *madal*.

1140. Cf., *Romeo and Juliet*, Act II Scene 2 Line 1: "He jests at scars that never felt a wound".

1151. The entire section except the first verse is addressed by the heroine to her friend. Even the first verse, which in the accepted text has *nin* meaning "your" has an alternative reading *tan* meaning "his". This is the translation here for the sake of consistency.

1157. A convention in ancient Tamil poetry was that separation from her lover makes a woman's hands thin and her bangles loose.

1181. Pallor is a marked change which overtakes a woman's complexion when separated from her lover. This plays a significant role in Tamil love poetry.

1203. A popular notion that sneezing is caused by someone thinking about you.

1208. Said in irony.

1209. "It is his cruel indifference, not his absence, which kills me".

1210. Lovers however far separated, both looking at the same moon, meet there. V.M. Gopalakrishnamachariar in this context refers to a *sloka* from Valmiki's *Ramayana*.

1252. Love, the offspring of the heart, puts his mother to work when all the world sleeps.

1257. The "we" is to include the friend who is surprised at the heroine's yielding to her husband.

1262. Addressed to her friend and with reference to future births.

1279. As much as to say that in his absence her bracelets will slide, and her shoulders grow thin and pallid. Her feet should help her by going with him.

1312. The usual formula to avert mishap. Cf., *gesundheit*.

1315. Thinking I didn't want her in my next.

1317. *Vide* 1203 and the note on it.

1330. The *Kural* begins with *a* the first letter of the Tamil alphabet and, in the most authoritative version, ends with *en*, the last letter.

FOR THE BEST IN PAPERBACKS, LOOK FOR THE

In every corner of the world, on every subject under the sun, Penguin represents quality and variety – the very best in publishing today.

For complete information about books available from Penguin – including Puffins, Penguin Classics and Arkana – and how to order them, write to us at the appropriate address below. Please note that for copyright reasons the selection of books varies from country to country.

In the United Kingdom: Please write to *Dept E.P., Penguin Books Ltd, Harmondsworth, Middlesex, UB7 0DA.*

If you have any difficulty in obtaining a title, please send your order with the correct money, plus ten per cent for postage and packaging, to *PO Box No 11, West Drayton, Middlesex*

In the United States: Please write to *Dept BA, Penguin, 299 Murray Hill Parkway, East Rutherford, New Jersey 07073*

In Canada: Please write to *Penguin Books Canada Ltd, 2801 John Street, Markham, Ontario L3R 1B4*

In Australia: Please write to the *Marketing Department, Penguin Books Australia Ltd, P.O. Box 257, Ringwood, Victoria 3134*

In New Zealand: Please write to the *Marketing Department, Penguin Books (NZ) Ltd, Private Bag, Takapuna, Auckland 9*

In India: Please write to *Penguin Overseas Ltd, 706 Eros Apartments, 56 Nehru Place, New Delhi, 110019*

In the Netherlands: Please write to *Penguin Books Netherlands B.V., Postbus 195, NL–1380AD Weesp*

In West Germany: Please write to *Penguin Books Ltd, Friedrichstrasse 10–12, D–6000 Frankfurt/Main 1*

In Spain: Please write to *Alhambra Longman S.A., Fernandez de la Hoz 9, E–28010 Madrid*

In Italy: Please write to *Penguin Italia s.r.l., Via Como 4, I-20096 Pioltello (Milano)*

In France: Please write to *Penguin Books Ltd, 39 Rue de Montmorency, F-75003 Paris*

In Japan: Please write to *Longman Penguin Japan Co Ltd, Yamaguchi Building, 2–12–9 Kanda Jimbocho, Chiyoda-Ku, Tokyo 101*

The House of Ulloa   Emilia Pardo Bazán

The finest achievement of one of European literature's most dynamic and controversial figures – ardent feminist, traveller, intellectual – and one of the great 19th century Spanish novels, *The House of Ulloa* traces the decline of the old aristocracy at the time of the Glorious Revolution of 1868, while exposing the moral vacuum of the new democracy.

The Republic   Plato

The best-known of Plato's dialogues, *The Republic* is also one of the supreme masterpieces of Western philosophy whose influence cannot be overestimated.

The Life of Johnson   James Boswell

Perhaps the finest 'life' ever written, Boswell's *Johnson* captures for all time one of the most colourful and talented figures in English literary history.

The Metamorphoses   Ovid

A golden treasury of myths and legends which has proved a major influence on Western literature.

A Nietzsche Reader   Friedrich Nietzsche

A superb selection from all the major works of one of the greatest thinkers and writers in world literature, translated into clear, modern English.

Madame Bovary   Gustave Flaubert

With *Madame Bovary* Flaubert established the realistic novel in France; while his central character of Emma Bovary, the bored wife of a provincial doctor, remains one of the great creations of modern literature.

FOR THE BEST IN PAPERBACKS, LOOK FOR THE

PENGUIN CLASSICS

ANTHOLOGIES AND ANONYMOUS WORKS

The Age of Bede
Alfred the Great
Beowulf
A Celtic Miscellany
The Cloud of Unknowing and Other Works
The Death of King Arthur
The Earliest English Poems
Early Irish Myths and Sagas
Egil's Saga
The Letters of Abelard and Heloise
Medieval English Verse
Njal's Saga
Seven Viking Romances
Sir Gawain and the Green Knight
The Song of Roland

FOR THE BEST IN PAPERBACKS, LOOK FOR THE 🐧

PENGUIN CLASSICS

Bashō	**The Narrow Road to the Deep North**
	On Love and Barley
Cao Xueqin	**The Story of the Stone** *also known as* The
	Dream of the Red Chamber (in five volumes)
Confucius	**The Analects**
Khayyam	**The Ruba'iyat of Omar Khayyam**
Lao Tzu	**Tao Te Ching**
Li Po/Tu Fu	**Li Po and Tu Fu**
Sei Shōnagon	**The Pillow Book of Sei Shōnagon**

ANTHOLOGIES AND ANONYMOUS WORKS

The Bhagavad Gita
Buddhist Scriptures
The Dhammapada
Hindu Myths
The Koran
New Songs from a Jade Terrace
The Rig Veda
Speaking of Śiva
Tales from the Thousand and One Nights
The Upanishads

End galley